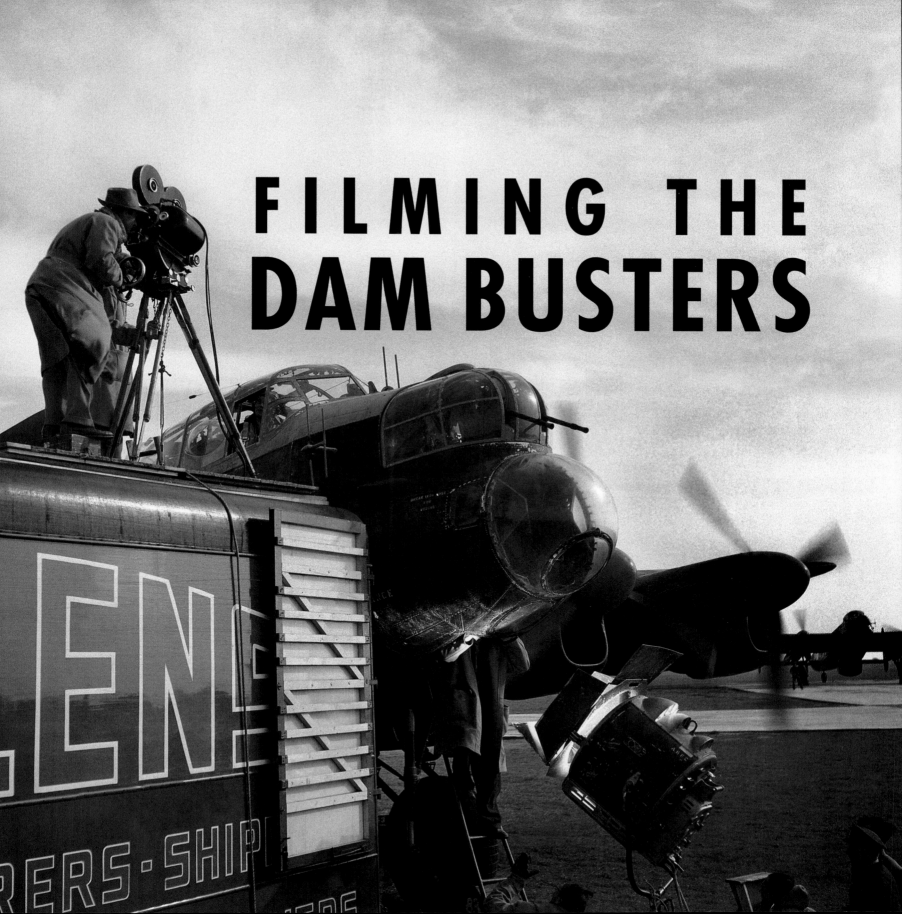

FILMING THE DAM BUSTERS

For my son,
Isaac

FILMING THE
DAM BUSTERS

JONATHAN FALCONER

FOREWORD BY RICHARD TODD

Sutton Publishing

First published in 2005 by
Sutton Publishing Limited • Phoenix Mill
Thrupp • Stroud • Gloucestershire • GL5 2BU

British Library Cataloguing in Publication Data
A catalogue record for this book is available from the British Library.

ISBN 0 7509 3712 2

Design and typesetting by Annie Falconer-Gronow
Printed in Great Britain by
J.H. Haynes & Co. Ltd, Sparkford.

contents

Foreword   7

Acknowledgements   8

Introduction   11

1   The Dam Busters – Fact   17

2   The Inspiration   33

3   The Cast   45

4   Men and Machines   63

5   The Aerial Filming   83

6   Main Filming and Post-production   121

Bibliography   151

Appendices

1   – The Credits   153

2   – The Aircraft in the Film   155

Index   159

Richard Todd pictured during a break from location filming on the Lincolnshire coast at Skegness.
Lincolnshire Echo

foreword

foreword

by

Richard Todd OBE

This is the second book by Jonathan Falconer to which I have had the pleasure of adding a foreword, and like his masterly treatment of the story of the dam busters themselves, *Filming The Dam Busters* is a meticulously researched and very readable story of the actual making of the film.

All the problems involved with preparation, filming and completion of a major movie such as *The Dam Busters* are graphically explained, and the difficulties that faced the director, Michael Anderson, make an engrossing study for readers interested in the background details of this or any other important film.

In addition to any normal filming hazards, such as stunt scenes, the very grave dangers encountered and overcome by the RAF crews during the flight sequences are gripping.

The details of the young cast involved, particularly those who went on to become famous, are really interesting. I found this an engrossing book.

Richard Todd
Grantham

acknowledgements

I am indebted to the following individuals and organisations for their help in the preparation of this book, and to whom my grateful thanks are due.

Tempe Brickhill, the daughter of Paul Brickhill, author of the book, *The Dam Busters*, for her interest in my research and for her generosity of spirit in answering my many requests for information; John Herron and his staff at Canal + Image UK Ltd, Pinewood Studios for kindly allowing me access to the photograph stills collection for *The Dam Busters*, and of course for permission to reproduce some of this wonderful collection here; Melanie Parker, Elmbridge Museum, Weybridge; the *Lincolnshire Echo*; the RAF Hemswell Association and Jeff Goodwin, editor of its journal *The Ermine Link*, for putting me in touch with some of those RAF personnel who took part in the filming; Ian MacGregor, The Met Office; Ray Bickel, Hucknall Library; Ian Thirsk, Curator of Film, RAF Museum; Frances Russell of the British Society of Cinematographers for enabling me to make contact with people from the film world; Daniel Crewe of *The Times* obituaries; Brian Goulding, co-author of the 'Lancaster at War' series of books; Dr John Sweetman, author of *The Dambusters Raid*.

From *The Dam Busters* film team: Michael Anderson, Director; Richard Best, Editor; Erwin Hillier, BSC, Director of Photography; Gilbert Taylor, BSC, Special Effects Photographer; Derek Browne BSC, Camera Operator, all of whom were generous with their help and time.

I am grateful to Richard Todd, who played the part of Guy Gibson in the film, for his interest in and support for this book, and of course for his foreword.

The aircrew: Mike Cawsey, flight engineer, 97 Squadron; James Fell, air signaller, 83 Squadron; Bill French, air signaller, 97 Squadron; Richard Lambert, pilot, 97 Squadron; Raymond McGee, instrument fitter, RAF Hemswell; Eric Quinney, pilot, 83 Squadron; Ken Souter, pilot, 83 Squadron; Ted Szuwalski, pilot, 97 Squadron; John West, air gunner, 83 Squadron. Thank you, gentlemen, for allowing me to quiz you mercilessly for your memories of the filming. It is sad to record the deaths of Ted Szuwalski in September 2004, Richard Best in December 2004, and Erwin Hillier in January 2005.

I owe particular thanks to Brian Goulding, Dr John Sweetman, Richard Best and Mike Cawsey for their help, freely given, in reading through my script, for their constructive comments, and for permission to use copyright photographs from their respective collections.

To everyone who has helped me, a very big thank you, for without you there could have been no book.

Jonathan Falconer

Bradford-on-Avon

Three aircrew from 97 Squadron had walk-on parts in the film. From left to right: Bill French, 'Chunky' Baines and Tug Wilson, with actors Tim Turner, Basil Appleby, Bill Kerr and unknown.
Bill French

Poster for *The Dam Busters*.
Canal Plus

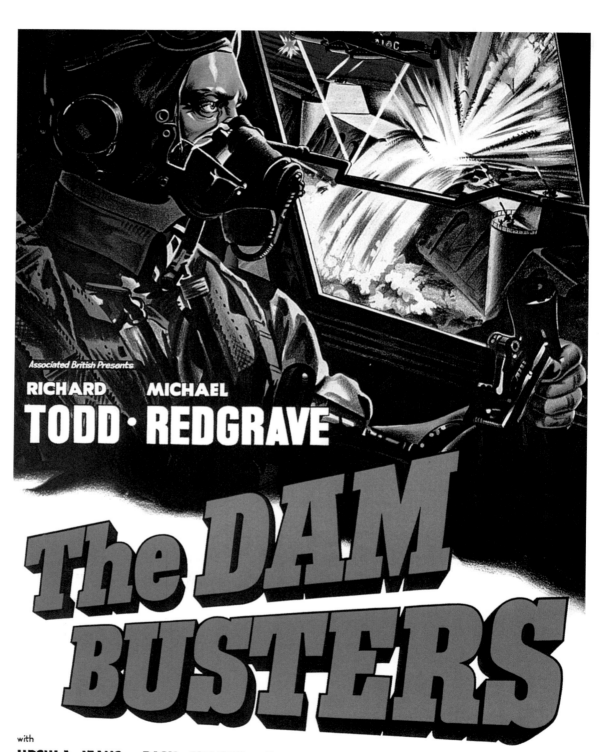

introduction

> "Praise and thanks to the pilots and crews that dared and risked so much so that the exploits of the dam buster heroes could be immortalised forever on film. It is fitting that these men should be mentioned and honoured . . . for recreating history."
> Michael Anderson, *Director*, **The Dam Busters**

For many cinemagoers, *The Dam Busters* is probably the best-known and loved British war film of the post-Second World War era. Based on W/Cdr Guy Gibson's own account in *Enemy Coast Ahead*, and Paul Brickhill's best-seller *The Dam Busters*, Michael Anderson's 1955 docu-drama recreates the tension and bravery of 617 Squadron's audacious raid on Nazi Germany's Ruhr dams in May 1943. Combining the quintessentially British qualities of inventiveness and dogged determination, the film is split into two distinct sections. The first deals with the fraught but ultimately successful development of Barnes Wallis's revolutionary bouncing bomb; the second deals with the raid itself and its subsequent impact on both the enemy and the airmen of 617 Squadron. Without falling into the traps of jingoism or sentimentality, Anderson's film celebrates the RAF's unsung heroes of the Second World War while at the same time highlighting Britain's tendency to stifle genius. The result is among the finest war films ever made.

The Dam Busters film was conceived and made against the background of an escalating Cold War when the threat of world annihilation through

'Any young pilot will tell you the best way to fly is low and fast, and if it is authorised, so much the better.' Dick Lambert, Lancaster pilot on the film.

Mike Cawsey/Garbett & Goulding Collection

introduction

nuclear confrontation was a very real possibility. In 1950, the human race teetered on the precipice of a third world war in Korea when Britain and the United States came into indirect conflict with the Soviet Union through the latter's military backing for North Korea. The coronation year of 1953 saw Avro Lincoln bomber crews from RAF Hemswell, who were despatched to the Far East in response to the ongoing Malayan Emergency, bombing Communist terrorists in their jungle hideouts. Some of these RAF aircrews were later to fly in the film. And in 1954, on a remote Pacific atoll called Bikini, the Americans detonated a hydrogen bomb in what was then the greatest-ever man-made explosion – 1,000 times more destructive than the A-bomb that had laid waste Hiroshima nine years earlier.

When filming for *The Dam Busters* began in 1954 it was not all doom and gloom, for it

Richard Todd as W/Cdr Guy
Gibson contemplates the
death of his Labrador dog,
Nigger, on the evening
before the dams raid.
Canal Plus E54.1.PROD.142

was in this year that Britons tasted 'fast food' at the first Wimpy Bar to open in London, and a 25-year-old trainee doctor named Roger Bannister became the first person to run a mile in under four minutes. 'Pretty Little-Black Eyed Susie' was the popular musical hit of the moment, and the football World Cup Final was played in Switzerland (which incidentally was also the only country that offered to host it) where West Germany beat Hungary 3–2.

In the fifty or so years since *The Dam Busters* was premiered in 1955 at the Empire cinema, in London's Leicester Square, surprisingly little has been published about the film, and in particular how and by whom the complex aerial filming work was carried out. In a way, this is all the more surprising because the dramatic flying sequences that were meticulously planned and stunningly photographed in monochrome by Erwin Hillier and Gilbert Taylor are central to the film's appeal and, arguably, up there with the very best war films featuring combat aircraft, like *Tora! Tora! Tora!* and *Top Gun.*

The process of filming three Lancaster bombers flying together in tight formation at low level, from a fourth aircraft, and often over water, is in itself a dangerous activity requiring the steady hands and keen eyes of film profession-als. Those RAF aircrew who skilfully flew the venerable Lancasters on camera deserve credit for their superb feats of airmanship that have brought alive the epic story of the dam busters to millions of viewers down the years. At the time they did not even receive screen credits for their part in the film, although the assistance of the Air Ministry and the RAF was duly acknowledged. They are the unsung stars of the film and deserve some measure of recognition alongside the memorable performances of Richard Todd and Michael Redgrave. In this book, the identities of these hitherto anonymous airmen are brought out of the shadows so they can be accorded the recognition that is their due.

Director Michael Anderson has this to say about his involvement in the film:

'Half a century later, I reflect that to have been chosen to make such a film, to have been associated with actors, great technicians and pilots of the Royal Air Force in the execution and re-creation of this daring raid in which so many lost their lives, is rewarding and humbling. And filled with memories and deep gratitude.'

During a break from location filming, an alfresco lunch is enjoyed by Ernest Clark (Air Vice-Marshal The Hon. Sir Ralph Cochrane), G/Capt Charles Whitworth (technical adviser), and Richard Todd (W/Cdr Guy Gibson), while director Michael Anderson looks on.
Canal Plus E54.1.PUB.136

1 the dam busters–fact

> Now there was no doubt about it; there was a great breach 100 yards across, and the water, looking like stirred porridge in the moonlight, was gushing out and rolling into the Ruhr valley . . . this was a tremendous sight, a sight which probably no man will ever see again.
>
> Guy Gibson, on breaching the Möhne dam, in *Enemy Coast Ahead*

On an unseasonably warm evening in May 1943, nineteen Lancaster bombers took off from an airfield in Lincolnshire and in the fast fading light headed out over the glassy North Sea towards the Dutch coast. Their targets were the great dams of western Germany, nestling in the wooded folds of the Ruhr hills some 300 miles distant. As the laden bombers thundered across the darkened landscape of enemy-occupied Europe, few among their 133 aircrew could have foreseen the legendary status that would attach to them in the years to come, or the collective nickname for their squadron that would soon become a watchword for bravery and daring – 'the dam busters'.

Squadron 'X' was formed by the RAF in great secrecy on 17 March 1943, with the specific task of breaching Germany's great hydro-electric dams

Après moi le deluge: the scene of devastation at the Möhne dam following the raid by 617 Squadron.
Bundesarchiv 1011/637/4192/23

In March 1943, W/Cdr Guy Gibson was posted to Scampton from commanding 106 Squadron to form and command a new and secret bomber squadron – 617 Squadron.
IWM MH6673

of the Ruhr. Reports from the British government's Ministry of Economic Warfare had predicted widespread chaos in Germany's industrial heartland if these dams that provided power for Nazi industry were destroyed. The one major difficulty in achieving this end was that hitherto the dam walls had been virtually unassailable from the air and were resistant to damage from conventional freefall bombs. Therefore, a means had to be found whereby a sufficiently powerful weapon could be delivered from the air and exploded against a dam wall in such a way as to cause a fatal breach of the structure.

Ten days later the squadron acquired its specific identity as 617 Squadron. Many of its aircrew were handpicked from existing squadrons in RAF Bomber Command's 5 Group by its highly experienced new commanding officer, W/Cdr Guy Gibson DSO & Bar, DFC & Bar. The blend of crews was truly international with 90 drawn from the RAF, 28 Canadians, 1 American, 12 Aussies and two from the RNZAF. Contrary to popular belief, not all were battle-hardened veterans or highly decorated. Some had flown two tours of ops, but many had not completed a first tour, and several were freshmen with little more than a handful of ops to their credit. For some of the flight engineers, the raid for which they were now training would actually be their first operation.

For some time, a British inventor named Barnes Wallis had been working feverishly on the problem of how to breach the Ruhr dams. As the Assistant

A date with destiny: W/Cdr Guy Gibson and his crew pause momentarily for the photographer before boarding their Lancaster, ED932, 'G' for George, on the evening of 16 May 1943.
IWM CH18005

Chief Designer of Vickers Armstrong's Aviation Section at Weybridge in Surrey, he was already an aeronautical engineer of considerable standing. After many months of research he had hit upon the novel idea of a bouncing bomb that could be dropped from a low-flying aircraft and skipped across the surface of a dam's reservoir, in much the same way as a flat pebble can be made to skim across the surface of water. (The only difference is that a pebble revolves around a vertical axis, whereas Wallis's bouncing bomb revolved around a horizontal axis.)

Codenamed 'Upkeep', his bouncing bomb is more accurately described as a cylindrical air-dropped mine. Back-spun at 500rpm it had to be dropped on to the reservoir from the very low level of

Barnes Wallis, the scientific
brain behind the bouncing
bomb.
Vickers

the dam busters – fact

60 feet by an aircraft flying at 220mph, and at a distance of some 1,275-1,425 feet from the dam's inner face. Skipping over anti-torpedo nets it would bounce across the surface of the water until it made contact with the dam wall. Sinking to a predetermined depth of 30 feet, three hydrostatic pistols each containing a primer charge would detonate, exploding the main charge of 6,600lb of Torpex explosive against the inner wall of the dam. The shock waves created by the explosion would crack open the structure, allowing the massive back pressure of millions of gallons of water to finish the job and pour into the valley below.

A modified version of the four-engine Avro Lancaster bomber that had entered RAF service in March 1942 was produced to carry the specially designed 'bouncing bomb'. It was designated BIII

Guy Gibson's Lancaster, 'G' for George, showing
the cut-away bomb bay with the Upkeep weapon
mounted between the pair of side-swing callipers,
and the belt drive to the weapon.
Crown Copyright

(Type 464 Provisioning). To enable the bomb to be carried, the Lancaster's mid-upper turret was removed and faired over, and the bomb doors in the belly of the fuselage were also removed. In the aperture that had been the bomb bay, the 9,250lb-bouncing bomb was held between a pair of side-swing V-shaped calliper arms. Power to spin the bomb (originally intended to operate the Lancaster's mid-upper turret and bomb bay doors) was transferred via a belt-drive from a variable-gear hydraulic motor mounted in the floor of the fuselage, and attached to one side of the weapon.

Photographic reconnaissance was vital to the success of the operation, which by now had been codenamed 'Chastise'. It provided crucial information to Bomber Command's planners about when the water levels in the reservoirs behind the dams had reached their maximum flood damage potential. It also gave important up-to-date intelligence on whether anti-aircraft defences had been strengthened on the dams themselves, and in the surrounding countryside.

On 7 February 1943, the first in a series of nine photo-reconnaissance (PR) sorties was flown to the Möhne dam and its reservoir by a Supermarine Spitfire of 541 Squadron from RAF Benson in Oxfordshire. At the time of the highest water flow in March, the Möhne reservoir contained some 176 million cubic yards of water and was the principal source of supply for the industries of the Ruhr valley 20 miles away. The winter weather was not kind to the recce pilots and not until the seventh attempt on 19 February was anything useful obtained for intelligence purposes from the photographic coverage. It took two further sorties, the last completed on 4 April, to provide enough photographs of sufficient quality for the planners. These were the same recce pilots who flew most of the sorties over the Ruhr dams. The intention was that they would get to know the dams and their hinterlands so well that when they flew the post-raid reconnaissance sorties they would be better able to notice any changes to the landscape made by the floodwaters.

Meanwhile, the crews of 617 Squadron trained intensively for six weeks, practising low-level flying by day and night to improve navigation skills and build confidence in flying safely over

Photo-reconnaissance sorties were flown over the Ruhr dams by the RAF's PRU Spitfires, beginning in early 1943. This is the Möhne dam and lake photographed in April, with the raid little more than a month ahead.
Crown Copyright

the dam busters – fact

water at low level. The cockpit windows of their Lancasters were coated with a special blue film which, when combined with amber filters fitted to the aircrews' flying goggles, gave a perfect simulation of moonlight during daytime. Practice attacks were made over the Derwent reservoir to help perfect their bombing technique before the operation itself.

On 5 April a request was made for photographic coverage of the Eder and Sorpe dams, which lay some 50 miles south-east and 6 miles south-west respectively of the Möhne. The Eder reservoir was bigger than the Möhne, containing more than 264 million cubic yards of water, which made it the largest in Germany. At the time of the raid, the Möhne and the Sorpe dams provided 75 per cent of the Ruhr's water require-ments. The final reconnaissance was completed on 15 May by Spitfires of 542 Squadron and the results of these recce flights, and the vital intelligence interpretations, were ready by mid-after-noon. In case the enemy suspected a raid on the dams, the PR pilots were briefed to cover a wide variety of targets in the Ruhr valley and further afield in Holland in the same sortie, so as not to draw undue attention to their real interest.

The first Lancaster BIII (Type 464 Provisioning) arrived at Scampton on 8 April, with the final aircraft being delivered on 16 May. On the night of 6/7 May, 617 Squadron flew a full exercise over the Eyebrook, Abberton and Howden reservoirs, Wainfleet and The Wash, simulating the attack planned for the operation itself. On the 11th, three crews flying modified Lancasters dropped inert-filled 'Upkeep' cylinders in the sea along the north Kent coast at Reculver, and on the 13th the only fully armed live 'Upkeep' to be spun and dropped before the operation was released from a Lancaster in a trial 5 miles off the Kent coast at Broadstairs. A full dress rehearsal by all 19 Lancasters was flown on the night of 14 May at Eyebrook reservoir (Uppingham) and Colchester's Abberton reservoir in Essex. On the afternoon of 15 May, 5 Group headquarters received the order from Bomber Command: 'Operation "Chastise". Immediate attack of targets X, Y and Z. Execute at first suitable opportunity.' The decision was taken to mount the attack the following night, 16/17 May.

Not until the main briefing for the operation in the early afternoon of 16 May were the crews finally notified of their targets after months of guesswork on their part. (The favourite was a precision attack on the battleship *Tirpitz*, which was holed up in a Norwegian fjord.) They were to strike at the great dams of western Germany, located east and south-east of the Ruhr. Nineteen Lancasters were to fly in three waves, the first comprising nine aircraft led by W/Cdr Guy Gibson, their target the Möhne dam. If that dam was success-fully breached, any aircraft whose bombs had not been dropped were to fly on to attack the Eder dam, some 50 miles away to the south-east. The second wave of five Lancasters led by F/Lt Joe McCarthy, an American, was actually to take off first and fly singly by way of a more northerly route to bomb the Sorpe dam. A third, 'mobile' reserve, wave of five Lancasters led by P/Off Warner Ottley was to take off two hours later and attack the last resort targets of the Diemel, Ennepe and Lister dams. But if the three main target dams had not been breached, they would be called upon to attack them.

Shortly before 2130hrs on the evening of 16 May 1943, the first of 19 Lancasters took off in three waves from RAF Scampton, each carrying a bouncing bomb beneath its belly. Initially, they climbed to 1,500 feet before descending to low level to traverse the North Sea, crossing the Dutch coast at 60 feet before making their way inland towards the Ruhr valley. Low flying was vital to avoid the attentions of German radar, flak and night fighters. One aircraft had already returned early after it struck the sea in a glancing blow that ripped off its bomb. This was P/Off Geoff Rice in AJ-H. Five more aircraft were shot down or crashed on the way to the target – P/Off Vernon Byers in AJ-K, F/Lt Bill Astell in AJ-B, P/Off Lewis Burpee in AJ-S, F/Lt Norman Barlow in AJ-E, and P/Off Warner Ottley in AJ-C. One more was badly holed by flak causing it to lose both its VHF radio and intercom, so its captain, F/Lt Les Munro (in AJ-W), turned for home without bombing.

Out of an initial force of 19 aircraft, this left 12 Lancasters to bomb the dams. W/Cdr Guy Gibson and four more crews (F/Lt John Hopgood, F/Lt

Bob Hutchison (wireless operator) and Guy Gibson exchange a few words before take-off for the dams raid.
IWM CH9682

Mick Martin, S/Ldr Melvin 'Dinghy' Young and F/Lt David Maltby) arrived over the Möhne dam at 0020hrs where they released their bombs in the midst of intense flak. Young succeeded in breaching its walls and on the fourth attempt at 0056hrs Maltby's weapon widened the breach that sealed the Möhne's fate and caused the structure to burst. Gibson then proceeded to fly the 50 miles and 14 minutes flying time to bomb the Eder dam, accompanied by F/Lt Dave Shannon (AJ-L), S/Ldr Henry Maudslay (AJ-Z), P/Off Les Knight (AJ-N) and with S/Ldr Melvin Young (AJ-A) as deputy leader. Thankfully, the dam was undefended but due to its geographical location in a deep valley surrounded by high hills, the Eder proved more difficult to bomb than the Möhne. After some ten attempts it was spectacularly breached by the bomb from Knight's Lancaster at 0156hrs. The Lancasters of F/Lt Joe

The Möhne dam, its walls torn wide open by the combined effects of 617 Squadron's bouncing bombs and millions of gallons of water.
Crown Copyright

(Opposite) Almost drained of water, this is the Möhne lake at the point where the road bridge crosses south of Delecke.
IWM CH9721

McCarthy (AJ-T), with F/Sgt Ken Brown (AJ-F) bombed the Sorpe dam. On the tenth and sixth runs respectively along the length of the dam wall they dropped their bombs in freefall (without spinning them), but the walls remained intact. The eleventh Lancaster piloted by F/Sgt Cyril Anderson was unable to find its target and with its rear turret disabled the aircraft returned to base at 0530hrs without dropping its bomb. The last aircraft to attempt an attack on a Ruhr dam in 'Chastise' was P/Off Bill Townsend in AJ-O. He dropped his

mine over the Ennepe dam on the fourth attempt, at 0337hrs, but failed to breach the wall.

The three Lancasters shot down after making their attacks were those of Maudslay (on the return flight near the German town of Emmerich, at 0236hrs), Young (also on the return flight, but crossing the Dutch coast at Castricum-aan-Zee, at 0258hrs), and Hopgood (whose Lancaster was damaged by flak and the blast from his 'Upkeep' weapon, and crashed at 0034hrs not far from the Möhne dam).

Only 11 Lancasters returned to Scampton as the dawn was breaking, with the final aircraft to arrive home touching down at 0615hrs. Eight Lancasters failed to return and 53 of their crew were killed, making it a costly operation in terms of men and aircraft, but to Bomber Harris and Sir Ralph Cochrane (AOC 5 Group) it was a price worth paying for the results achieved. For his bravery in leading the raid and for drawing the attention of the defending flak gunners at the Möhne dam away from subsequent attacks by his pilots, Gibson was awarded the Victoria Cross. In the words of his award citation: ' . . . he personally led and displayed, as is usual with him, the highest valour in the face of deliberately sought and tremendous additional risk . . .'. Thirty-three other aircrew received gallantry decorations for the parts they had played in the successful prosecution of the raid, making 617 Squadron the most decorated unit in Bomber Command.

Breaching the Möhne and Eder dams was a huge achievement. The millions of gallons of water that poured forth from the breached walls, at rates of up to 70,000 cubic feet per second,

inundated nearly 40 miles of valleys and caused the deaths of more than 1,300 people. In fact, the effects of the flooding were felt elsewhere in Germany, more than 300 miles away. Steel production in the factories of the Ruhr was affected for the remainder of the year, pumping stations became silted up by the floodwater; roads, railways and canals were severely disrupted, and agriculture and food supplies suffered from the flooding. Had the Sorpe dam also been breached, the repercussions for Ruhr industry and civilians living close by would have been even more severe.

At home, the morale of the British people received a boost when it heard news of this major feat of arms. A true and accurate assessment of the damage could not be measured until after the war had ended, but when the British Bombing Survey Unit investigated it revealed that the effects of the dams raid on German industry were not as dire as had been predicted. But the success of the raid lay in its wider implications: the huge fillip it gave to British morale at a time when it was really needed; and in the considerable achievements, both in terms of design

Back from the dams: some of Gibson's exhausted crew are debriefed in the early hours of 17 May by 617 Squadron's intelligence officer, S/Ldr Townson, as Bomber Harris and Cochrane look on.
IWM CH9683

technology and airmanship, that enabled the RAF to achieve the hitherto unimaginable. The image of the RAF was further enhanced in the eyes of its own political masters and those of its American ally, by its ability to strike at and destroy a previously untouchable strategic target, using a small force of highly trained aircrew to deliver their weapons with pinpoint accuracy.

When the Axis forces in North Africa finally surrendered to the Allies in the wake of the victory over Rommel at El Alamein in October 1942, the corner had finally been turned for Britain. No more defeats. The destruction of the Ruhr dams in the following spring was one of a series of vital strategic and pro-

The King visited Scampton on 27 May to meet the crews of 617 Squadron.

paganda victories for the Allies that would culminate in the Normandy landings a year later on 6 June 1944, effectively spelling the beginning of the end for the Nazi enslavement of Europe.

the dam busters – fact

2 the inspiration

> "The secret of the film's success and longevity is Sherriff's script. It was perfect in its construction, dialogue and imagination."
> Richard Best, *Editor*, **The Dam Busters**

In 1945, after six years of bitter conflict, the Second World War finally came to an end. It was in May that the Third Reich was eventually brought to its knees and its generals forced to surrender unconditionally to the victorious Allies. But in the Far East it took three more months of vicious fighting before the Japanese finally submitted in August. Yet, it still took the deadly force of two atomic bombs to make them see the writing on the wall.

With the war now over, a whole host of personal war stories were just waiting to be told. It was not long before the first of the autobiographies by the RAF's wartime high commanders and squadron bosses hit the bookstalls. Bomber Command's contribution to winning the war was marked by W/Cdr Guy Gibson's classic *Enemy Coast Ahead*, published posthumously in 1946, followed in 1947 by Marshal of the RAF Sir Arthur Harris's *Bomber Offensive* and Air Vice-Marshal Donald Bennett's *Pathfinder* in 1958.

Not to be outdone, the film-makers made a significant contribution to the wartime lore of the RAF. Terence Rattigan's *The Way to the Stars* (1945) and Philip Leacock's *Appointment in London* (1953) highlighted on the big screen the part played by the men of Bomber Command during the war years. But arguably one of the most famous British war films must be *The Dam Busters*, combining stiff upper-lip performances, British design ingenuity and strong storyline in full measure.

Eleven years after the Ruhr dams raid, 617 Squadron's remarkable exploit was turned into a blockbusting Associated British Picture Corporation film, starring Michael Redgrave as Barnes Wallis and Richard Todd as Guy Gibson. Based largely on Paul Brickhill's best-selling book, *The Dam Busters*, to this day it has remained one of the most enduring war films of all time, thanks in part to the understated way in which the story is told.

This was not the first time that a film had been proposed about the dams raid, because late in 1943 an American idea to make a Hollywood movie about the raid was considered by the Air Ministry and the Ministry of Information. However, British reluctance to divulge specific operational details to the Hollywood studio, not to mention strong criticism of the script from, among others, Barnes Wallis, meant that the plan came to nothing. With what we know today about Hollywood's ques-

tionable interpretations of war stories, this was probably a good thing.

In the summer of 1950, Ealing Studios had expressed an interest in making a film about the dam busters story, but discussions with studio director Sir Michael Balcon came to nothing. In the end the film option was signed with Associated British in November 1951.

The inspiration for the Associated British film was a best-selling book called *The Dam Busters* by a young Australian newspaper journalist-turned-author named Paul Brickhill, and Guy Gibson's own account of the raid in his classic *Enemy Coast Ahead*. Actually it is just the first half of Brickhill's book, and a handful of chapters from *Enemy Coast Ahead*, that describes the dams raid. Brickhill had relied heavily on Gibson's account as a source, and combined it with his own extensive interviews with surviving air and ground crews from 617 Squadron. In his book *The Dam Busters*, Brickhill readily acknowledges the debt he owed to Guy Gibson who ' . . . wrote some of the wonderful story of this affair towards the end of his excellent *Enemy Coast*

Guy Gibson

Alongside Leonard Cheshire, Guy Gibson is probably the most famous RAF bomber pilot of all time. Precocious, arrogant, and with an unrelenting enthusiasm for operations, he went on to win undying fame for his role in leading the attack on the Ruhr dams in May 1943 for which he was awarded the Victoria Cross. Gibson flew operationally from the day war was declared, completing 177 operational sorties with few breaks over the five years before his final fatal flight in September 1944.

Born in India on 12 August 1918, he was commissioned into the RAF in 1937 and his first posting was to 83 Squadron as a bomber pilot. His early career in the Service was undistinguished but the war was to change all that. Completing his first tour in August 1940, Gibson was posted to instruct at an Operational Training Unit before transferring to Fighter Command and a posting to 29 Squadron flying Beaufighter night fighters. In ninety-nine operational sorties he claimed three enemy aircraft destroyed and was promoted to squadron leader with a bar to his DFC on completion of his tour in December 1941. After a short spell instructing he was posted back to Bomber Command and given the command of 106 Squadron. He completed his second bomber tour in March 1943 as a wing commander, DSO and Bar, DFC and Bar, before he was told to form 617 Squadron on 21 March. He led nineteen Lancasters on the famous dams raid on 16/17 May in which the Möhne and Eder dams were successfully breached, and for which he was awarded the VC. Gibson remained with the squadron until August when he was officially taken off operations.

Between then and D-Day he became a celebrity figure at home and in the USA, a protégé of Winston Churchill, a prospective Conservative Party candidate for Macclesfield, and the author of what later became a best-selling account of the bomber air war, *Enemy Coast Ahead*. However, he was desperate to get back to operational flying and in September 1944 'Bomber' Harris finally relented. Gibson piloted a 627 Squadron Mosquito as master bomber in a raid on Rheydt/Monchengladbach on 19 September, but on the return journey his aircraft inexplicably flew into the ground in Holland and exploded, killing Gibson and his navigator Squadron Leader James Warwick.

W/Cdr Guy Gibson's account of the dams raid in *Enemy Coast Ahead* was an inspiration for the film.

W/Cdr Guy Gibson, whose personal account in *Enemy Coast Ahead* of the formation and training of 617 Squadron, and of the dams raid itself, proved an invaluable source to Paul Brickhill when researching his own book.
IWM CH13121

the inspiration

Ahead. Any full account must draw on this and I am grateful for permission to do so, in addition to my own researches.'

In 1950, Brickhill had been approached by Air Chief Marshal the Hon. Sir Ralph Cochrane, the Vice-Chief of the Air Staff, to write the wartime history of 617 Squadron. Back in 1943, Cochrane had been the Air Officer Commanding, 5 Group, and was closely involved with the planning and execution of the dams raid. The book he proposed was not to be a formal history as such, but in Brickhill's words 'more of the human story of the squadron'.

Paul Brickhill was ideally suited to writing the wartime story of 617 Squadron. His time as a reporter with the *Sydney Sun* before the war had taught him how to interview to get at the facts, how to write clearly and succinctly in short sentences, and that he should never use the passive tense in preference to the active when telling a story through someone else's eyes. But it was Brickhill's subsequent experience as a wartime RAF fighter pilot and established author that led Cochrane to settle on him for the task. It was a wise choice because Brickhill's natural flair for

telling a good story well saw *The Dam Busters* transformed from an informal squadron history into a worldwide bestseller by the time the film rights to the book were optioned by Associated British in 1951.

Unbeknown to Paul Brickhill, the founder wartime adjutant of 617 Squadron, Harry Humphries, had been keeping notes and gathering information on the squadron with a view to one day writing his own account of the dam busters. When Humphries received a

In 1950, Air Chief Marshal The Hon. Sir Ralph Cochrane, Vice-Chief of the Air Staff (who had been the wartime commander of 5 Group, Bomber Command), commissioned Paul Brickhill to write a history of 617 Squadron, which was later called *The Dam Busters*. He carefully vetted Brickhill's draft of the book and predictably advocated cutting or toning down any passages that showed officialdom and the RAF in an unsympathetic light.
IWM CH14564

Paul Brickhill's *The Dam Busters* became an international best-seller.

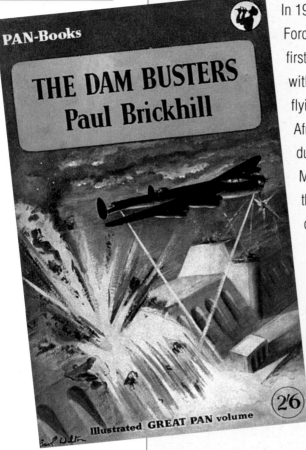

PAN-Books

THE DAM BUSTERS
Paul Brickhill

Illustrated GREAT PAN volume

2'6

Paul Brickhill

In 1940, at the age of twenty-four, Paul Brickhill joined the Royal Australian Air Force and trained in Canada as a fighter pilot before coming to England where first he flew Spitfires with 74 Squadron. In 1942 he arrived in North Africa with 274 Squadron flying Hurricanes, then moved to 92 Squadron flying Spitfires. Twice shot down and wounded during his spell in North Africa, Brickhill's flying career came to an abrupt end in March 1943 during operations against the German Mareth Line. He was jumped by a Messerschmitt Bf109 over the Tunisian desert and shot down. Wounded in the attack, he managed to bale out of his stricken fighter. His parachute drifted on the wind and he landed in a minefield from where he was picked up by the Italians. Brickhill was duly handed over to the Germans and shipped off to Germany as a prisoner-of-war where he wound up in Stalag Luft III.

'As it turned out,' he said in a postwar interview, 'the wind was a friendly one for it blew me, half-conscious, into German hands – and captivity. I call it "friendly" because it was from what I experienced of prisoner-of-war life that I was able to write *Escape to Danger*, the book that seems to have set me up.'

It was in this notorious camp at Sagan, set among the pine forests of what had been East Prussia, that he became involved with the escape organisation that planned the mass break-out of 76 men in March 1944, although luckily for Brickhill he was not among them. All but three of the escapers were recaptured, and 47 of them were executed by the Gestapo on the direct orders of Hitler. *The Great Escape*, published in 1951, was Brickhill's first book on his own (he had co-authored with Conrad Norton, *Escape to Danger*, published in 1946) and described his experiences at Sagan that culminated in the so-called Great Escape. His second and perhaps most celebrated book, *The Dam Busters*, was published later the same year. By Christmas it had sold 50,000 copies in Britain alone and was well on the way to becoming a best-seller. It was followed in 1954 by *Reach for the Sky*.

Paul Brickhill's credentials as a newspaper journalist and wartime RAF fighter pilot convinced Cochrane he was the right man to pen the history of 617 Squadron.

Tempe Brickhill

The screenplay for *The Dam Busters* by the acclaimed English playwright R.C. Sherriff is regarded by many as the magic ingredient that has given the film its perennial appeal and longevity.
Elmbridge Museum, Weybridge

letter from Brickhill asking for some assistance with anecdotal details of squadron life, he felt as though he was being asked to give up his 'right' to the story, and declined to help. This became something of an issue between the two men and it took the personal intervention of Leonard Cheshire to persuade Humphries to provide Brickhill with the information he sought.

Associated British bought the film rights to *The Dam Busters* so that Richard Todd (who was then in the middle of a seven-year contract to the company) could play the part of Guy Gibson. The film company paid an advance of £7,500, which was shared equally between the author and the screenplay writer, R.C. Sherriff. The overall budget for the film was some £200,000, which was a large sum for a British film of the 1950s. (Today, this is the equivalent to £3.2 million and would be considered a low-budget film.) But as might be expected, the big American films of the same period were commanding budgets of £1 million and more.

Michael Anderson, who was relatively unknown in the film world at the time,

was picked to direct the film. It was his first major picture although he was later to win acclaim for directing *Around the World in Eighty Days* (1956), *The Quiller Memorandum* (1966), and *Logan's Run* (1976). Richard Todd remembers the day when Robert Clark, Director of Production, told him about the appointment of a young man whom he'd never even heard of as director. *'I thought, "Oh, no, they're going to spoil the ship for a ha'porth of tar". I later had dinner with him [Anderson] at the Café Royal and I was won over by his knowledge and ability, and his quiet, sensible manner. On set, he never got flustered, was always in control and had terrific authority. Michael Anderson <u>made</u> The Dam Busters.'*

Michael Anderson recalls: *'I had had the good fortune, as assistant director to the great David Lean, to work on and be mostly in charge of many aspects in the making of Noel Coward's great naval film, In Which We Serve [1942]. To the extent that when my call-up papers came through during the making of the film, Lord Terrington asked Lord Mountbatten personally to arrange for my exemption from service until the film was finished. This was granted. But I had learned and used planning and organisational skills that were to be projected into the making of The Dam Busters. I had also learned from the Masters themselves that you cannot do it alone. You must surround yourself with the right people.'*

Anderson chose to approach the story in a documentary style and to film it in monochrome, thereby giving a hard-edged grittiness that colour stock would have failed to achieve. It also enabled original wartime film footage of bouncing bomb test-drops to be seamlessly inserted into the new feature film. Richard Best, the film's editor, has this to say about Anderson's choice of mono-chrome: *'To use colour would have been detrimental. It is too glamorising and distracting. Black and white some-how distils the essence of character and scene.'*

The screenplay was by the famous British playwright R.C. Sherriff, author of the acclaimed play *Journey's End* (1928), which was based on his own experiences in the trenches during the First World War. In common with Paul Brickhill, the one-time insurance claims adjuster used his war service as a captain in the East Surrey Regiment on the Western Front to inform his own writing. Like Brickhill, he too had been wounded in action – in the case of Sherriff at Ypres in 1917, and severely – and as such his understanding of the fighting man makes his screen adapt-ation of Brickhill's book all the more convincing.

Richard Best believes that Sherriff's screenplay was the vital ingredient in the film: *'Apart from the other facets of production that were excellent – casting, acting, directing, design, lighting, music, etc – the secret of this film's success and longevity is Sherriff's script. It was perfect in its construction, dialogue and imagination.'*

Work on the script for **The Dam Busters** began in earnest late in 1951 and a full first draft of Sherriff's screen-play was available in August 1952. Writing to Barnes Wallis on 21 November, production supervisor Bill Whittaker presented him with a copy of the script for his comments, and described the challenges experienced by Associated British in scripting and designing the film:

'You, more than anyone, will appreciate, that in the whole of this great story there are several phases which would, in themselves, form the basis for a complete picture and our main difficulty has been to contain within the bounds of one film a balanced presentation of the whole achievement. This has involved careful selection and, in places, perhaps a somewhat simplified treatment of highly complicated issues. If there appears at times to be over simplification it is because we have so little time in which to make clear to an uninstructed audience, without giving them too much to digest, just what the problems were and how they were overcome. In this we were also hampered by the security restrictions.'

The 'somewhat simplified treatment' to which Whittaker refers embodies several points of fact that relate to the dams and to the raid itself. In the aircrew briefing scene the script mentions the Möhne, Eder and the Sorpe dams as the targets for 617 Squadron, although in 1943 the squadron was briefed to attack a total of six dams (the other three being the Ennepe, Lister and Diemel). In 1943, there were three waves of aircraft involved in the attack, but the film mentions only the first wave. Attacks on the Möhne and the Eder are shown but not that on the Sorpe. There is a good reason for omitting the latter because it remained unbreached despite the best efforts of two Lancaster crews. Defeat for the RAF was something the film-makers did not wish to include. The film is also misleading in its reference to the Möhne, Eder and Sorpe as being Ruhr dams. While it is true that the Möhne and the Sorpe are both on tributaries of the River Ruhr, the Eder was entirely unconnected to them in both geographical and strategic senses, being on a tributary of the Fulda, and used for water management purposes rather than for feeding industry in the Ruhr valley. Between them, the Möhne and the Sorpe provided 75 per cent of the Ruhr's water requirements and had both dams been breached the impact on the Ruhr's industrial infrastructure would have been immense, and far more disruptive than the combined effects of the breaches in the Möhne and Eder dams.

Born into an acting family in London, Michael Anderson, began his distinguished film career as a production runner at Elstree Studios in 1936. He later joined the Associated British Picture Corporation and was chosen to direct *The Dam Busters*, a film for which he continues to hold great affection.

Canal Plus E54.1.PUB.84

There followed a further, lengthy, period of discussion with various interested parties and certain revisions were made to the script in order to make the film as realistic as possible. Drafts were also sent out in January 1954 to aircrew survivors of the dams raid and the next of kin of RAF airmen who had died in the raid, for their comments. Additional expert technical advice was on hand from Barnes Wallis (he paid many visits to Elstree Studios during the film's production), as well as from 'Bomber' Harris, the Hon. Sir Ralph Cochrane (AOC 5 Group in 1943), Mick Martin (skipper of 'P' for Popsie) and Gp Capt J.N.H. Whitworth (station commander at Scampton in 1943). Final adjustments were made to the script and by April 1954 *The Dam Busters* was all set for the main shooting to begin.

3 the cast

> When the film actors came onto the base in RAF uniforms, for about a week or more we were saluting them. We then realised who they really were . . .
>
> SAC Raymond McGee, RAF Hemswell

Director of Productions at Associated British, Robert Clark, bought the film rights to Paul Brickhill's book so that Richard Todd could play the part of Guy Gibson. Although at the time he was a leading film actor, it was the first modern war film for which Todd had been cast, and his characteristically understated portrayal of Gibson is perhaps typical of this actor's approach.

In common with Paul Brickhill and R.C. Sherriff, Richard Todd had also experienced combat at first hand, although in a conversation with the author he denied that this experience in any way informed his interpretation of the role of Gibson. *'There were quite a few of us on the film who had been in the services and knew how to march and how to salute,'* he said. *'We felt comfortable in uniform.'* Todd began his acting career in repertory theatre in 1937, but with the outbreak of war in 1939 he volunteered for the Army, serving initially in the King's Own Yorkshire Light Infantry. In 1944, as a captain, he was assistant adjutant of 7 Para and parachuted into Normandy in the early hours of D-Day with 6th Airborne Division near Pegasus Bridge. For *The Dam Busters*, Todd carefully researched the persona of Gibson, talking

Many observers commented that the personal resemblance between Richard Todd (right) and Guy Gibson (below) was uncanny. Todd made a point of studying his subject and even went as far as adopting the non-regulation German *Schwimmvest* life-jacket and Boy Scout bracelet favoured by Gibson during the war.
Canal Plus E54.1.PROD.23 and IWM CH11047

to those in 617 Squadron like Mick Martin who had known him, and to Gibson's father and Barnes Wallis. The close physical resemblance between Todd and Gibson is striking, with one film reviewer (who had also known Gibson) commenting that Todd was 'extraordinarily like the late wing commander'.

Todd went on to enjoy a highly successful career on stage and screen, and latterly in television where he has

The thespian and the matinee idol: Michael Redgrave and Richard Todd at RAF Scampton.
Ted Szuwalski

The birth of the bouncing bomb theory: Michael Redgrave as Barnes Wallis experiments in his garden with catapult, marbles and a tin bath full of water. This is clearly a studio set, but the original experiments were carried out by Wallis in the garden of his home, White Hill House, at Effingham in Surrey.
Canal Plus E54.1.PROD.111

starred in such small screen dramas as *Midsomer Murders* and *Holby City*. His other war film credits include *D-Day the 6th of June* (1956), *Yangtze Incident* (1957), *The Long and the Short and the Tall* (1961), *The Longest Day* (1962), and *Operation Crossbow* (1965).

Michael Redgrave played the other

lead alongside Richard Todd. He saw himself primarily as a stage actor, and strongly rejected notions of being referred to as a film star, although ironically he was to go on to make more than fifty films. In 1954, because of three classical seasons at Stratford and the Old Vic, his finances were not in good

On location with the main unit shooting crew, probably on the Lincolnshire coast, near Skegness, at Gibraltar Point. Richard Todd and Michael Redgrave look out to sea for the test aircraft to drop its prototype bouncing bomb.
Canal Plus E54.1.PUB.145

Barnes Wallis meets his screen likeness, Michael Redgrave.
Canal Plus E54.1.PUB.169

shape and so he relied upon his agent to find him whatever work he could. The result was a string of six films in succession that included *The Dam Busters* and with it the part of Barnes Wallis. Redgrave met Wallis in person and made a point of visiting his drawing office and the Vickers-Armstrong works at Weybridge to observe the behaviour of the design team who worked there. This clearly enabled him to give a highly

At RAF Scampton, aircrew walk to their pre-op briefing. Bill Kerr is on the left.
Ted Szuwalski

(Opposite) Michael Anderson on set directing Bill Kerr as F/Lt Mick Martin. Kerr was perhaps better known to 1950s radio audiences in Britain as the Aussie from Wagga Wagga in *Hancock's Half Hour.*
Canal Plus E54.1.PUB.85

filming the dam busters

individual portrayal of the character of Wallis on screen. Redgrave's other war film credits include *The Way to the Stars* (1945), *The Sea Shall Not Have Them* (1954), *The Heroes of Telemark* (1965), and *Battle of Britain* (1969).

Director Michael Anderson remembers his first meeting with Barnes Wallis: *'He tried to explain the theory of the bomb to me, but suddenly realised that it was still on the secret list. "Oh dear," he exclaimed, "I can't possibly tell you*

John Fraser (left), who also
enjoyed some success as a
pop singer in the 1950s,
played the part of F/Lt John
Hopgood whose Lancaster
was shot down and crashed
close to the Möhne dam.
Canal Plus E54.1.PROD.18

the cast

any more. I've probably said too much already." And he scrunched up the paper he was writing on and threw it into the waste-paper basket. *Then he looked aghast at the pad he had taken the paper from. "Dear me, my wife will never forgive me. I just used a sheet of her best notepaper."* And he gave me the wry Barnes Wallis smile that Michael Redgrave so aptly portrayed in the film.'

From the viewpoint of the 'real' servicemen at RAF Scampton, the actors were easily recognised about the station, as James Fell recalls:

'*Although they were wearing RAF uniform, they were the only ones wearing built-up shoes! Some looked the part like Richard Todd, who was superb as Guy Gibson. Bill Kerr was excellent as Mickey Martin. Bill immediately swapped his shiny new service cap for the "50-mission" hat that belonged to one of our navigators. Bill, whose ears had "chocks" slipped behind them by the make-up department so as to make them stick out like the real Mickey Martin, also sported an RAF handlebar moustache. He was invariably saluted by young airmen when walking about the station*

Better known to 21st-century television audiences as Inspector Wexford in the Ruth Rendell murder mysteries, in 1954 George Baker played the part of F/Lt David Maltby in *The Dam Busters*.
Canal Plus E54.1.PUB.179

the cast

and his reply to them was "don't be such a silly ****" which was a source of much confusion to them and not quite the thing for good order and discipline.'

Bill Kerr had starred in the Bomber Command film drama *Appointment in London* (1953) as F/Lt Bill Brown, but he was to become much better known to British radio and television audiences of the fifties as the Aussie from Wagga Wagga in *Hancock's Half Hour*.

A certain amount of confusion had reigned at Scampton and Hemswell in the first weeks of filming because it was almost impossible to distinguish the film actors from the real RAF personnel, as SAC Raymond McGee recalls: *'When the film actors came on to the set in RAF officers' uniforms, for about a week or more we were saluting them. We then realised who they really were and orders were issued that the actors had to wear an armband when not film-ing to show they were with the film unit.'* Just to confuse matters further, some RAF personnel were used as extras. Ken Souter and his aircrew who flew the Lancasters on film acted as extras when they attended the main

raid briefing scene at Scampton in order to make up the numbers.

Although Corporal Tom Bailey's name does not appear anywhere in the film credits, he enjoyed a certain measure of fame with his contemporaries at RAF Hemswell for his walk-on part as Guy Gibson's sergeant ground crew chief. When Gibson (Richard Todd) and his crew arrive at the dispersal point after final briefing to board 'G' for George, Gibson asks 'How is she, sergeant?', to which Bailey salutes and replies 'Bang on, sir!' Soon after the film came out Tom Bailey was promoted to sergeant, but his new-found fame came at a price. For many months afterwards, wherever he went on the base, he was greeted mercilessly with the words 'Bang on, sir!'

Ted Szuwalski remembers that the principal actors, Michael Redgrave and Richard Todd, were not allowed to fly with them in the Lancasters, presumably for insurance reasons, a fact confirmed by Richard Todd in an interview with the author. *'The minor actors were allowed to come with us if they were not required on set,'* recalls Ted. *'I enjoyed meeting and talking to the film stars, but*

Redgrave wasn't that talkative.'

The filming attracted a lot of attention from service personnel and the general public alike. Indeed, the families of personnel serving at Hemswell and Scampton would go up to the airfields on Sundays to watch the filming. James Fell recalls an amusing incident: *'A very pretty young girl asked which one was Richard Todd. One of the actors immediately pointed out Bill Kerr and said he was Todd, and that he would be very pleased to meet her. So it came to pass that it was not always the luck of the leading man to get the girl.'*

In most conflicts the fighting is done by young men, and so it was during the Second World War: most of Bomber Command's aircrew were in their late teens and early twenties. It was important, therefore, that the actors cast to play 617's aircrew in the film should be young-looking in order for them to appear credible. Of these, Nigel Stock was 34, George Baker 25, and Robert Shaw 27 years old when the film was being made. With this age requirement, many of those eventually cast for *The Dam Busters* were relatively unknown to the cinema-going public at the time,

although several did go on to achieve fame and recognition as film and stage actors.

P/Off 'Spam' Spafford, Gibson's bomb-aimer, was played in the film by Nigel Stock. He had started his stage career as a boy actor at the age of 12 and played several juvenile parts in the West End and the Old Vic. During the Second World War he fought with the Indian Army in Burma and China, was twice mentioned in despatches, and ended the war as a major. After the war he enjoyed a successful career in film, television and theatre. Not long before *The Dam Busters*, he had starred alongside Bill Kerr in *Appointment in London*. He is probably best remembered for his television portrayal of Dr Watson in the Sherlock Holmes stories, and for playing the part of another television doctor, Owen MD, in the series of the same name from the early seventies.

George Baker, who plays F/Lt David Maltby, is better known to audiences today as television's Inspector Wexford in the Ruth Rendell mysteries. In 1953 he had been talent-spotted at the Haymarket Theatre by director Guy

(Opposite) Robert Shaw (left) played Gibson's flight engineer Sgt John Pulford. As Quint the shark hunter in the film *Jaws*, Shaw became well-known to cinema audiences of the mid-1970s.
Canal Plus E54.1.PROD.94

In one of several examples of the film-maker's artistic licence, while watching a London show, Guy Gibson was supposed to have come up with the idea of the twin spot lamps fitted to the undersides of the Lancasters to gauge their height above water. Richard Todd and Basil Appleby are pictured among the girls of the dancing troupe who appeared in the show on the film.

Hamilton and offered a part in his film *The Intruder*. From that he got *The Dam Busters* which earned him a seven-year contract with Associated British.

Robert Shaw played the part of Gibson's flight engineer, Sgt John Pulford, but he and Todd did not hit it off which led for a strained relationship on set. *'We weren't chummy; we simply just didn't get on. In fact, he didn't really get on with anyone on the film,'* says Richard Todd. Shaw went on to enjoy an international film career with credits that included *A Man For All Seasons,*

Nigger enjoys some attention from Richard Todd and Patrick Barr (Mutt Summers) during a break from filming.
Canal Plus E54.1.PUB.26

Back from the dams: Guy Gibson (Richard Todd) climbs down the crew ladder to join his crew.
Canal Plus

From Russia With Love, Battle of Britain, The Taking of Pelham One Two Three and *Jaws*. Sadly, his career was cut short when he died from a heart attack at the tragically young age of 51 in 1978.

Of the other members of Gibson's crew in the film, Brewster Mason (F/Lt Dick Trevor-Roper) went on to become a Shakespearean actor, Anthony Doonan (F/Lt Bob Hutchison) later starred in the television series *Man in a Suitcase* and *The Persuaders*, and Brian Nissen (F/Lt Torger Taerum) pursued a dual career as a screenwriter and actor.

NIGGER

One of the most memorable stars of the film was not a human actor, but a black Labrador dog named Nigger. In real life Guy Gibson had owned a black Labrador by the same name and in the film the part of Nigger was played by an Army mine-detector dog whose real name was also Nigger. Richard Todd, who was a dog-lover, remembers how his best friend on the set was certainly Nigger:

'Bill Whittaker weeded him out of the Army, complete with his corporal handler. A dog will only answer to one master so I asked that his Army handler be relieved of the job and so I took over complete control of Nigger. On the first day he joined me I was at the White Hart Hotel in Lincoln where I was resident during the filming at Scampton. He was a kennel dog so I was terrified he'd lift his leg when he was inside the hotel. Fortunately he was good. I was allowed to keep him with me at the hotel so long as he didn't go in the dining room. My hotel bathroom had a tiled floor so this was ideal in case he had any problems. I gave him an old duffel coat which became his talisman. It accompanied him wherever we went and it was where he slept or lay down. Nigger worked wonderfully for me. The day came when the Army wanted him back and I had to leave him. We had been together for three months and had developed a strong bond.'

'Not here, boy.' An RAF SP sends Nigger on his way from the camp gates at Scampton.
Canal Plus E54.1.PROD.62

(Overleaf) The name of Guy Gibson's dog is considered distasteful to many in the politically correct 21st century, but it is of its time. This has led to some television companies feeling the need to edit his name out of recent broadcasts of the film.
Canal Plus E54.1.PUB.195

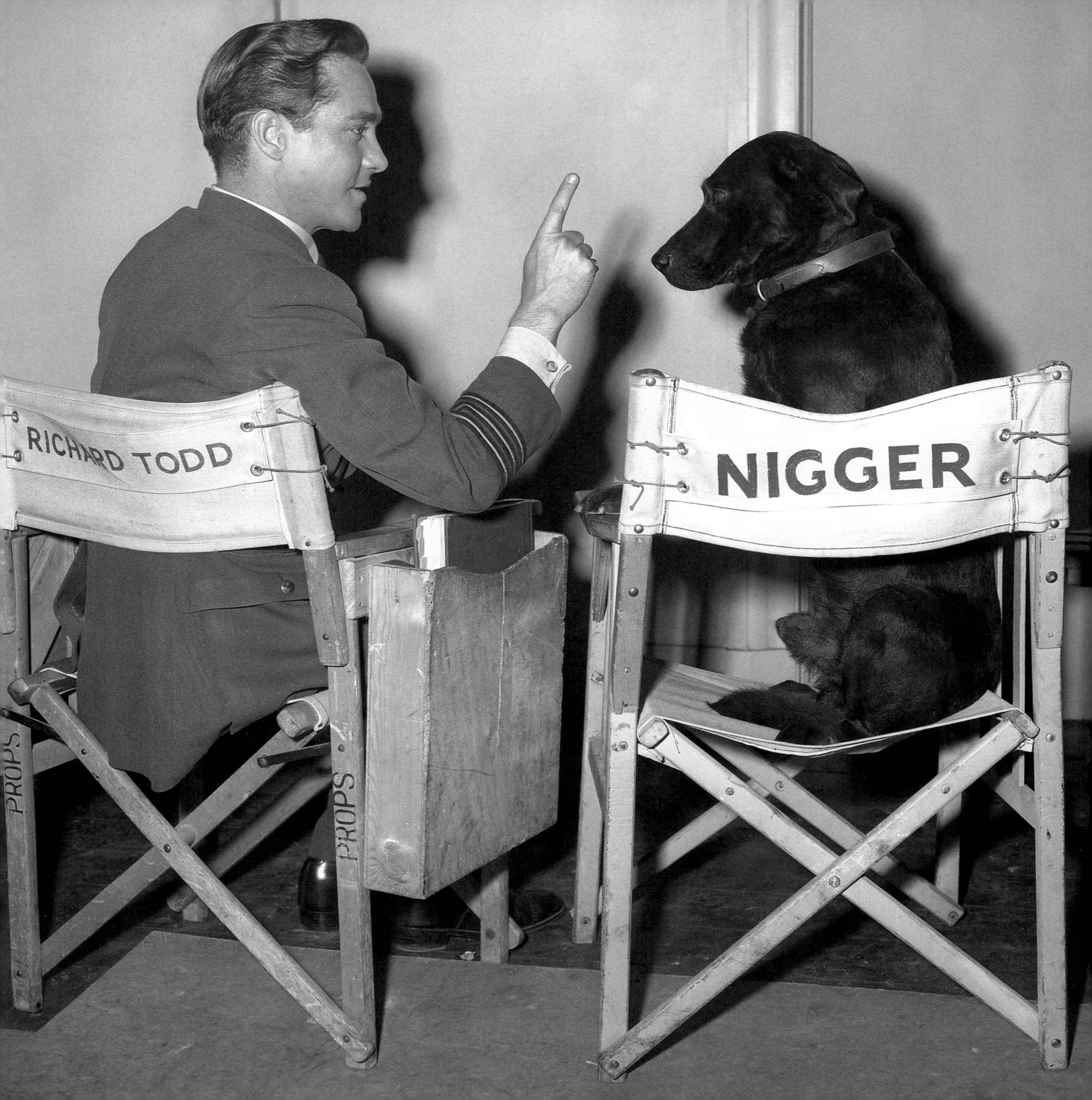
RICHARD TODD
NIGGER
PROPS
PROPS

4 men and machines

> In 1954, the Air Ministry charged the film company £100 per engine hour running time for the Lancasters, Wellington and Varsity. At today's prices, it would cost an estimated £1.5 million just to operate the four Lancasters for the film.

In 1941, a young Pole named Ted Szuwalski escaped from the harsh regime of a Soviet Gulag. After trekking halfway around a world at war, he finally arrived in England in 1944 where he joined the RAF and trained as a pilot. The war ended before Ted could complete his flying training and he was soon demobbed, but he rejoined the Air Force in 1949. His third operational posting was in July 1952, to Hemswell, where he joined 97 Squadron on Lincolns. Ted can remember the day he was picked to fly in *The Dam Busters*:

'The Wing Commander Flying at Hemswell called me into his office and told me I was going to be flying on The Dam Busters film. On a recent detachment to the Suez Canal Zone I had flown my Lincoln at deck height alongside a ship that was sailing down the Suez Canal. I could recall seeing the passengers on the deck waving across at me, I was flying that low. When I landed my squadron commander asked to see me and said there had been a complaint of dangerously low flying made against me by the captain of this

Four Avro Lincoln pilots from RAF Hemswell were picked to fly the Lancasters in the film. These Lincolns are from 97 Squadron and are pictured in 1954 over the Lincolnshire countryside, having recently returned from a detachment to the Far East.

Mike Cawsey

ship. *Strangely, nothing was ever done about it. This may have been written up in my personal records and could well have worked in my favour since it might explain why I was picked for the film!'*

Associated British needed pilots who could fly the Avro Lancaster, but the venerable bomber had been withdrawn from RAF frontline service in 1950 to be replaced by its larger and more powerful successor, the Avro Lincoln. The Lincoln was a development of the Lancaster and had many common features, so it was logical that its pilots would be the obvious choice to crew the Lancasters for the Associated British production.

Four operational Lincoln crews from 83 and 97 Squadrons at nearby RAF Hemswell were picked to fly the Lancasters on camera. Most of these men were fresh from a four-month detachment to Singapore as a part of Operation Bold (air strikes against the

Communist terrorists in Malaya). They were led by F/Lt Ken Souter, a flight commander on 83 Squadron, who was ably supported by pilots F/Sgt Joe

Cameron (of 83), and Sgts Mike Cawsey and Dennis Wheatley (of 97). In addition to the Lancaster flying, the crews continued to be involved in the regular

Some of *The Dam Busters* film aircrew photographed in 1954 against the backdrop of one of the Lancasters. From left to right: F/Sgt Miles (signaller), F/Sgt Jack Worthington (engineer), F/Lt Ken Souter (pilot), F/Off Colin Batchelor (navigator), Sgt Mike Cawsey (engineer), F/Sgt Ted Szuwalski (pilot), F/Sgt Jock Cameron (engineer), F/Sgt Joe Kmiecik (pilot), and Sgt G.W. Wrightson (air gunner). Absent from this photograph are pilot F/Off Dick Lambert and his flight engineer Sgt Dennis Wheatley.
Garbett & Goulding Collection

Kmiecik AFM (83 Squadron), and F/Off Dick Lambert and F/Sgt Ted Szuwalski (97 Squadron). Three flight engineers were picked to fly with the four pilots, since usually only three of the four Lancasters would be operating at any one time. They were F/Sgt Jock

squadron commitments, flying their Lincolns on Cold War exercises by day and night throughout the summer. This included 4 or 5-hour cross-country exercises over Europe as well as many hours of continuation training to stay 'current' on the Lincoln.

Tadeusz (Ted) Szuwalski was one of two Polish NCO Lincoln pilots serving with the RAF who were picked to fly the Lancasters in the film. The other was Jerzy (Joe) Kmiecik. Ted is pictured in the cockpit of one of the film Lancasters. At the end of filming in October 1954, Ted turned his back on fixed wing flying and retrained as a helicopter pilot.

Ted Szuwalski

As an interesting aside, Guy Gibson started the Second World War as a Hampden bomber pilot with 83 Squadron. Several of the original dam buster crew captains also came from 97 Squadron – F/Lts David Maltby, Les Munro and the American Joe McCarthy.

Usually, it was only the pilots and engineers who were required to fly the Lancasters for filming duties, particularly if it was only on local flying. But for the longer trips to the Lake District a navigator was carried as well as additional crew members, such as air gunners and air signallers. Understandably, there was never a shortage of people who wanted to hitch a ride in one of the Lancasters during the aerial filming sorties, such was the popular fascination at Hemswell and Scampton with the making of the film.

Ken Souter was chosen to lead the RAF aircrew for the film. *'A request was sent from the film company to the CO of the unit,'* recalls Ken, *'who handed it down to the squadron commander who in turn selected me to lead the aircrew chosen for the film.'* Ken already had some fifteen years' experience behind him as a pilot. He had joined the RAFVR in 1939, training as a fighter pilot. Shortly after the Battle of Britain he was posted to 43 Squadron and later saw action in North Africa where he flew Hurricanes with 73 Squadron. Ken left the RAF in 1946 to pursue a career in civil aviation in South Africa, but he returned to England in 1950 where he rejoined the RAF and his first posting was to 83 Squadron on Lincolns. Mick Marriott, a navigator on the same squadron, remembers Ken as 'a brilliant pilot and a very laid-back individual'.

Joe Kmiecik was Polish and had flown Spitfires and Mustangs in action with 303 Squadron during the Second World War. Like his fellow countryman Ted Szuwalski, he had made a remarkable escape from a Soviet Gulag in 1941 and eventually made it to England where he joined the RAF and learned to fly. Joe qualified as a fighter pilot and continued to fly operationally with the RAF from 1944 right up to his retirement as a flight lieutenant in 1981. Eric Quinney remembers him as *'the finest pilot that I ever came across. He taught me all that I know about close formation flying in large aircraft.'*

Dick Lambert joined the RAF in 1942, but due to everlasting delays in his flying training he missed the war by a matter of months. His first posting was to 101 Squadron as a sergeant pilot. He was commissioned in 1950 and later joined 97 Squadron. *'One day in 1954 I was returning to RAF Hemswell after a spot of leave and was amazed to see four Lancasters and a Wellington parked by 97 Squadron's hangars. Little did I know that I was to be attached to the film unit. The catch, of course, was that I still had to fly normal squadron details.'*

Ken Souter was chosen to head up the Lancaster crews for the film. He was a highly experienced RAF pilot who had flown Hawker Hurricanes operationally during the Second World War with 43 and 73 Squadrons. Ken returned to England from frontline service in North Africa for treatment of a chronic ear infection. The Sunderland flying boat in which he was a passenger was routed via Portugal which was a neutral country, so to smooth his passage home Ken was compelled to masquerade as a non-combatant – in his case a vet.
Ken Souter

It was often the practice for flight engineers and other crew members to take turns at the controls during flights to gain basic flying experience in case of an emergency that might incapacitate the pilot. Here, Dick Lambert's flight engineer, Dennis Wheatley, takes a turn 'on the pole' during filming.
Dick Lambert

Eric Quinney, from 83 Squadron, replaced Dick Lambert when he was posted away from Hemswell late in the filming schedule during August. *'I did not get involved in the early stages as my squadron commander [S/Ldr W.C. Sinclair AFC] was loath to have too many of his pilots involved because the squadron's normal operational commitment still had to be met. I eventually got my chance as the result of much badgering of the CO by F/Sgt Joe Kmiecik, and I started flying on 7 August 1954.'*

Eric remained in the RAF and continued to fly until 1968 when he left the Service, having achieved the rank of Master Pilot (aircrew warrant officer).

For many, the stars of the film are undoubtedly the Avro Lancasters themselves. It is hard to believe that Lancasters were in short supply when the filming commenced in April 1954. (One RAF unit still operating the Lancaster at this time was the School of Maritime Reconnaissance that flew GR3s from St Mawgan in Cornwall.) Four Mk 7 aircraft were taken out of storage at 20 Maintenance Unit, RAF Aston Down, and specially modified for the film.

'We heard a rumour that the squadron was to get a couple of Lancasters for making a film of the story of 617 Squadron on the dams raid,' recalls James Fell, who at the time was a 23-year-old air signaller on 83 Squadron at RAF Hemswell. *'Like all service rumours, in good time it became fact and in due course four Lancasters arrived from a maintenance unit and were unceremoniously parked at the far side of the airfield.'*

These were NX673, NX679, NX782

S/Ldr W.C. 'Bill' Sinclair, the commanding officer of 83 Squadron (left) and his wife, pictured with F/Lt Dick Lambert and his wife at a squadron function towards the end of the filming.

Dick Lambert

On location at Scampton, the dummy bouncing bombs are delivered to the airfield amid tight security. In a novel departure from their 'day jobs' of Lancaster flying for the film, F/Off Dick Lambert (seen here on the right, looking underneath the tarpaulin) and his flight engineer, Sgt Dennis Wheatley, had walk-on parts as RAF SPs on gate guard duty. 'We had to stop the trucks with the new bombs arriving, lift up the covers and say "Well, I've never seen a bomb like that before!". You've no idea how many ways you can say that!' says Dick Lambert.

Canal Plus E54.1.PROP.31

Sergeant James Fell, an air signaller with 83 Squadron, flew on a number of filming sorties.
James Fell

A rare photograph of all four of the film Lancasters grouped together. ZN-G is NX782, the only Lancaster to be retained as a standard Mk 7 for filming.
Ted Szuwalski/Mike Cawsey

and RT686. In fact, '673, '679 and '782 had already developed a taste for the movies because they had recently starred in Philip Leacock's feature film about a wartime Lancaster squadron, *Appointment in London*, which was premiered in 1953.

For Associated British it was an expensive business to lease the four Lancasters for filming. The Air Ministry charged the company £100 per engine hour running time, and as there were usually three Lancasters, the Varsity camera aircraft and/or the Wellington involved (3 x 4 engines and 2 x 2

Lancaster RT686 is run up on the tarmac at RAF Hemswell early on during filming. The white identity codes seen here were soon repainted in the correct wartime red.
Mike Cawsey/Garbett & Goulding Collection

engines), £1,600 per hour in the early 1950s was no small sum. *'I have to admit that we saved the film company thousands by not entering the nature of the flight in the flight authorisation log until after the sortie,'* remembers Sergeant Pilot Eric Quinney of 83 Squadron. *'If no filming took place for any reason, we entered the flight as "continuation training" – ergo, nothing to do with the film company.'*

Today, this sum is equivalent to £1,620 per engine hour, or £6,480 per Lancaster per hour. The total bill for the use of the four Lancasters and their crews would be an estimated £1.5 million at today's prices. (For the purpose of comparison, it cost the makers of **Dark Blue World** (2001), a film about Czech Spitfire pilots in the wartime RAF, some £5,300 per hour per Spitfire for filming.)

To make them resemble as closely as possible the actual Lancaster B III (Type

This plan view of one of the film Lancasters reveals the hastily applied camouflage scheme on the upper fuse-lage and wings. This had been done some years earli-er in preparation for the appearance of three of *The Dam Busters* aircraft in the film *Appointment in London* (1953).
Canal Plus

464 Provisioning) aircraft that flew on the dams raid in 1943, three of the Mk 7s (NX673, NX679 and RT686) were specially modified at Hemswell by a working party from the A.V. Roe Repair Organisation at Bracebridge Heath. They had their mid-upper gun turrets (Glenn Martin Type 250 CE23), H2S radomes and bomb-bay doors removed to convert them to the authentic dam buster configuration. The bomb-bay itself was further modified to create the rebated aperture from which the mock-up of the bouncing bomb was suspended.

However, the bomb itself was still on the secret list when the film was being made (it was only declassified in 1963), so the resulting mock-up bore little resemblance to the real thing. Made out of plywood and plaster of Paris, the slab-sided bouncing bomb mock-up for the film was somewhat larger in overall size than the real weapon, and deeper, which accentuated its shape and low-slung appearance for the benefit of the camera. The wooden replica was winched up into position in the bomb bay recess and secured to the aircraft by bolts. Being firmly attached to the Lancaster's belly, the replica bomb was never intended to be dropped.

NX782 was retained as a standard Mk 7 and painted to represent Guy Gibson's own aircraft, ZN-G, when he commanded 106 Squadron in 1942–3. Coded IH-V, this aircraft had previously been flown in *Appointment in London* and was usually captained by the commanding officer of 148 Squadron, S/Ldr Lofty Hayes.
Mike Cawsey/Garbett & Goulding Collection

NX679 banks away from the camera of flight engineer,
Mike Cawsey, showing to advantage the absence of mid-
upper gun turret and the modified bomb-bay complete
with dummy bomb.
Mike Cawsey/Garbett & Goulding Collection

With its twin Bristol Hercules engines developing full take-off power, Vickers Wellington T10, MF628, skims over the heads of the second unit camera team on the runway during filming.
Canal Plus E54.1.PUB.155

The upper surfaces of the aircraft and fuselage sides were then over-painted in the standard wartime European theatre night bomber camouflage of dark green and dark earth (albeit rather crudely if compared to wartime factory-applied camouflage), with code letters in red, to cover the black and grey-white paint scheme that was introduced by the RAF in late 1945 for bombers serving in the Far East. The undersides of the fuselage retained their night black scheme, although the underwing aircraft serial numbers were painted out.

men and machines

A busy scene at Scampton as Michael Redgrave and Patrick Barr (centre) are filmed by the second unit crew. In the background are the film's four Lancasters and on the right Mosquito PR35, VR803. With evidence of at least four Canberra bombers in the background (one behind the first Lancaster, and three behind the Mosquito), it can be appreciated just how difficult it was for the camera operator to keep non-film aircraft out of shot.
Canal Plus E54.1.PUB.140

Purists will notice a number of differences between wartime Lancasters and the Mk 7s that appear in the film. Perhaps the most obvious is the Frazer-Nash FN82 power-operated rear turret that was equipped with twin Browning .50-inch machine guns. In 1943, the Lancasters of 617 Squadron would have been fitted with FN20 rear turrets armed with four of the less-potent .303-inch Brownings. In addition, the series of small windows along each side of the fuselage that were a noticeable feature of wartime Lancasters were deleted from the postwar Mk 7. And note, too, the absence of the engine exhaust manifolds that would have been present on wartime Lancasters to reduce glare and suppress sparks from the hot exhausts at night.

The film aircraft wore different squadron code letters on either side of the fuselage, thereby enabling three Lancasters to play the parts of six on screen. NX679 was painted to represent Guy Gibson's ED932 AJ-G and it was the only aircraft to have its serial number altered for the film. The other Lancasters retained their official RAF serials. NX673 was painted in the markings of Mick Martin's P-Popsie (ED909 in 1943). One Lancaster, NX782, was retained as a standard Mk 7 and painted as ZN-G to represent Gibson's aircraft when he commanded 106 Squadron, before being called upon to form 617 Squadron in March 1943. NX782 was the Lancaster that appears in the training flight flying sequences prior to Operation Chastise. There are some memorable moments in the film of this aircraft performing at extremely low level over Lake Windermere and the Derwent dam, skilfully flown by either F/Sgt Joe Kmiecik or Ted Szuwalski.

Other aircraft that had 'walk-on' roles in the film were Vickers Wellington T10, MF628, and de Havilland Mosquito PR35, VR803. The Wellington appears briefly in the early part of the film taking off for a test air-drop of the mine, but most of the footage that purports to feature her is in fact archive film of a Wellington Mk II shot over Chesil Beach near Weymouth during the early tests of the actual prototype bouncing bombs in January 1943. Because the appearance on screen of MF628 was short, it was decided to keep the Wimpy in her silver Training Command livery instead of

Without pomp or ceremony, the film's four Lancasters were flown out of Hemswell in October 1954 as discreetly as they had arrived almost seven months before.
Canal Plus E54.1.PUB.122

repainting her in the standard wartime night bomber camouflage of black, dark green and dark earth. Occasionally, she was used as an air-to-air camera platform with the camera operator seated in the aircraft's rear turret. At the time of filming in 1954, MF628 was the only flying example of the Wellington extant and today she can be seen on static display at the RAF Museum, Hendon.

Mosquito PR35, VR803, is seen briefly – and only – on the ground as the backdrop to Mutt Summers after he has flown one of the test-drop sorties. It is linked to archive footage that appears on the film of a Mosquito BIV testing the 'Highball' (anti-ship) bomb although it purports to be a test-drop of an 'Upkeep' weapon, which it is not. In fact, the Mosquito was never used for testing 'Upkeep', nor did Mutt Summers ever fly a Mosquito for the purposes of testing the bomb. VR803 was something of a rarity, however, since she was one of just a handful of Mosquito B35s that were converted to a photographic-reconnaissance configuration.

In a further example of the film company's simplified treatment of the dam busters story, in 1943 there were several other test pilots from Avro and Vickers, in addition to Mutt Summers, who also carried out trial weapon drops, but from modified Lancasters as well as from Wellingtons. This is not covered in the film.

Although there was engineering support for the Lancasters at Hemswell and Scampton, when it came to the supply of spare parts it was necessary for an aircraft to be despatched north to 22 MU at RAF Silloth in Cumbria. *'At the time of making the film, the MU was engaged in breaking up Lancasters,'* recalls flight engineer Mike Cawsey. *'Whenever we needed a part this is where it came from, taken off one of the aircraft in the graveyard. This was a very sad sight – engines cut off and lying on the ground, instruments smashed with a hammer and airframes reduced to aluminium waste for recycling as saucepans.'*

Once filming had been completed, the four Lancasters that had helped to recreate the epic dam busters story were returned from whence they came to 20 MU at RAF Aston Down. Mike Cawsey remembers that *'after the Battle of Britain displays at Anthorn*

(Cumbria) and Biggin Hill in September, we did not fly the Lancs any more and they disappeared from Hemswell as mysteriously as they had arrived.' Pilot Eric Quinney's flying logbook records that on 6 October 1954 he made the 'return flight of NX673 to Aston Down MU'. The RAF Scampton station diarist also noted that 'the Lancasters flew from the station for the last time to satisfy a BBC television commitment', an activity which has not been identified.

At Aston Down the Lancasters languished awhile until declared surplus to requirements and then, without ceremony, they were cut up and sold to the British Aluminium Co. in July 1956 to be melted down for scrap.

5 the aerial filming

In 1943, the Lancasters of 617 Squadron flew at exactly 60 feet over the Ruhr dams to release their bouncing bombs. During filming in 1954, 60 feet looked a lot higher when the rushes were viewed. So for much of the low-level work the crews flew at 40 feet.

The RAF put Scampton aerodrome at the disposal of Associated British as its base for the main shooting, which started early in April 1954, and a spell of good weather meant initially that filming could proceed unhindered. The second unit aerial filming was undertaken at a number of English locations that included the RAF airfields at Hemswell, Scampton, Kirton-in-Lindsey, Syerston and Silloth, and continued throughout the summer until its completion in mid-September.

Director Michael Anderson describes how he handled the task that faced him with the aerial filming: *'My main objective, in conjunction with producer Bill Whittaker, was to choose the right people, delegate authority, trust in those chosen and let them do their job. Then, with the editor, to review their work in the overall context of the way I saw the film, make such additions and corrections as were necessary on a day to day basis, and make sure that all of the material needed in the final film was shot. I cannot praise Erwin Hillier, Gilbert Taylor and Richard Best too highly for their*

Location filming for *The Dam Busters* generated a huge amount of interest from service personnel and civilians alike, both on and off the bases at Hemswell and Scampton. This busy scene shows a great deal of activity, centred on a main unit crew shooting a Lancaster cockpit scene in NX679 from the roof of a pantechnicon that is doubling as a camera platform, while RAF personnel and their families look on.
Canal Plus E54.1.PUB.132

contributions in shooting and editing the flying sequences for the film. They took responsibility and chances that were above and beyond the call of duty.'

Under the overall control of the Director of Photography and Aerial Photography, Erwin Hillier, much of the superb aerial footage was filmed by Associated British's second unit team led by the Special Effects Photographer, Gilbert Taylor, from a twin-engined RAF Vickers Varsity, WJ920, on loan from the

Bomber Command Bombing School, Lindholme, and flown by F/Lt Scowan. Some of the air-to-air footage that required head-on shots of the Lancasters was taken from the rear turret of Wellington T10, MF628, flown

RAF Hemswell was the Lincolnshire bomber airfield out of where most of the flying sequences were flown. At the time of the filming, Hemswell was home to five Lincoln and Canberra squadrons. In this photograph can be seen three Lincolns, the Varsity camera plane, two Lancasters and the Wellington. In the background is a mixture of Lincolns and the two other Lancasters. This airfield was the subject of the wartime film *Night Bombers*, filmed – unusually – in colour by Hemswell's station commander, Air Commodore Iliffe Cozens, during 1943.

Mike Cawsey/Garbett & Goulding Collection

Planning a shot: George Blackwell (special effects model unit), Bill Whittaker (production supervisor), and Robert Jones (art director) use a scale model and viewing glasses to set up the shot of a Lancaster crossing the enemy coast. In the pre-computer age, such planning was a very time-consuming and laborious process. On the wall behind can be seen a large photographic print of the breached Möhne dam and its rapidly emptying lake.
Canal Plus E54.1.PUB.50

This photograph of the Varsity's flight deck shows how the left-hand pilot's seat had been removed, along with the cockpit side window, to facilitate filming. The pilot flies the aircraft from the co-pilot's seat.
Canal Plus

(Opposite) Wellington T10, MF628, was used as an additional camera platform for the air-to-air cinematography, and also starred in the film in its own right during the initial trials of the bouncing bomb. This aircraft is one of only two surviving Wellington bombers in the whole world and can be seen at the RAF Museum, Hendon.
Canal Plus E54.1.PUB.146

by F/Lt 'Butch' Birch. The Wimpy also starred in the film in its own right as the aircraft from which the early tests of the bouncing bomb were conducted. Gil set up all of the flying sequences himself and personally did as much as 50 per cent of the aerial photography, assisted by Val Stewart and Norman Warwick. *'We had a lot of very early or very late calls to fly,'* remembers Gil. *'Having an Associated British camera crew we never had problems with the times. The pilot of the Varsity was a most talented*

chap and the Lanc crews loved the break from service flying.' The Lancasters were flown on camera by pilots Ken Souter, Joe Kmiecik, Ted Szuwalski, Dickie Lambert and latterly Eric Quinney.

To facilitate filming, the metal floor of the Varsity was replaced by one made of wood, to which were attached camera tripods and grips. The aircraft's nose section was also modified to take a forward-looking camera. A further two cameras were installed inside the aircraft, one beside the rear port side

Scampton and Hemswell

In 1954, RAF Hemswell was a frontline operational airfield, home to five bomber squadrons flying Lincolns and Canberras. RAF Scampton was also operational, with four Canberra bomber squadrons in residence. In 1954 Scampton was a Master Diversion Airfield and as such was required to be open around the clock, seven days a week, fielding a huge number of aircraft movements. The choice of Scampton as the main RAF station for location filming was significant. It had been the wartime base of 617 Squadron, from the unit's formation in March 1943 until it moved away to RAF Coningsby in the August.

Gil Taylor, Norman Warwick and Val Stewart, dressed in full flying kit, operate the camera from inside the Varsity camera plane, while the flight deck crew look on. Hopefully, somebody was up front at the controls!
Canal Plus

cargo access door and the other in the left-hand seat of the cockpit for which the cockpit window had been specially removed, the pilot flying from the right-hand seat.

Mitchell and Arriflex cameras were

used by Hillier and Taylor to film *The Dam Busters*. *'The trademark of good cinematography'*, says Gil Taylor, *'came from the American Mitchell-type cameras which were a prerequisite for serious film work.'*

Joe Kmiecik and Jock Cameron give the victory salute from the cockpit to photographer Mike Cawsey. Despite the evident fooling around, as a pilot Joe Kmiecik was among the finest Avro Lincoln pilots in the RAF and was eagerly sought after for his daring low-level flying display routines at air shows at home and abroad. Ironically, Joe survived a Soviet Gulag followed by thirty years of operational flying with the RAF, only to die in a sense-less DIY accident at his home in Gibraltar in 1992.
Mike Cawsey/Garbett & Goulding Collection

Michael Anderson remembers the important part played by Art Director Bob Jones in planning the aerial filming: *'With me, he spent many weeks breaking down the script into the smallest component parts, storyboarding each flying sequence and putting a sense of calm and order into what might have been chaos.'*

Most of the flying sequences were flown out of Hemswell during the week, and from Scampton at the weekends, with the aircraft returning to Hemswell at the end of each day's filming. The second unit film crew and its equipment was transported to Scampton and the other locations where it was required in an Airspeed Oxford (PH462) flown by F/Lt Caldwell, and in another Varsity (WJ912) flown by P/Off Mathieson.

Each time the Lancasters flew it was for some sort of filming activity: take-offs,

With the sound of twelve mighty Merlins threshing the air, a vic of three Lancasters beats up Scampton during filming. On the ground can be seen a station flight Tiger Moth and Oxford.
Canal Plus

formation flying, low flying and landings, but the greater part of their flying was done in formation. On one session, the crews were briefed to practise wheeler landings and rolling off them, which was not an activity they were used to in their regular service on Lincolns.

F/Lt Ken Souter recalls that as a team they didn't really have any practice as such, but went more or less straight into the filming. Sergeant Air Signaller James Fell, who was in F/Sgt

Joe Kmiecik's crew, remembers how they got to grips with the Lancaster: *'I had 1200 hours in my log book, I'd just bought my first car, a Wolseley 18, spring had arrived, and my crew was fortunate to be one of those chosen to take part in the filming of the low-level flying scenes and to act as extras. Life was looking good.*

'In April we embarked on a pro-gramme of low-level flying. There was

no official conversion course so we were given a copy of the Pilot's Notes and told to learn on the job. Some years previously we had spent three months at 230 Operational Conversion Unit (OCU) at RAF Scampton learning the systems of the Lincoln, which were similar to the Lancaster, followed by some 76 hours of flying to make us conversant with the type.'

In the film a Lincoln or two can be seen on at least one occasion in the background, although the last Lincoln unit (230 OCU) was disbanded at Scampton in October 1952, re-forming at RAF Upwood in the following August. It would not have been un-known for Lincolns from other units to visit Scampton on occasions, particularly as it was an Emergency Diversion Airfield.

Sgt Mike Cawsey, who was Ted Szuwalski's flight engineer, recalls: 'For our familiarisation we had a look at the Pilot's Notes, examined the aircraft inside and out, ran the checks a couple of times and made sure we could start the engines. I had to get my First Line Servicing Certificate signed up to say I was competent to do the necessary when away from base.'

Two of the Lancaster crews who flew extensively during the filming, from April through to September 1954: Sgt Mike Cawsey, F/Sgt Jock Cameron, F/Sgt Joe Kmiecik, and F/Sgt Ted Szuwalski.
Garbett & Goulding Collection

Tucked in close together, RT686 (M) and NX679 (G) approach Scampton's runway (background, far left). Located four miles north of Lincoln, Scampton was the first of a number of airfields built on the rise known as the Lincoln Cliff (centre right) running north on the west side of the A15.
Mike Cawsey/Garbett & Goulding Collection

Jim Fell clearly remembers some of the defining moments of his first training flight in a Lancaster: *'It was apparent from the start that the Lancaster was more responsive than its larger and heavier younger sister the Lincoln. On our first flight we flew out over the North Sea for low-level handling trials. I can clearly recall looking up at some gentlemen fishing at the end of Skegness Pier as we flashed past them. That morning, I learnt that if you got down low enough over water the propellers would whip up a spray. Our training for the film contin-*

ued alongside our normal squadron duties and in due course the film crew and the actors arrived at RAF Scampton.'

Mike Cawsey recalls his first familiarisation flight in a Lancaster and the flying practice that followed: *'On 9 April 1954, Ted and I flew up to RAF Lossiemouth in NX782 and stayed for lunch. We then brought it home again, nearly five hours flying, and I had an hour on the pole [at the control column]. That was the sum total of our training. Three days later we were on low-level runs over the Derwent*

Dam and lake. On 20 April in one hour of night flying [actually twilight], we used the 'V' landing lamps under the fuselage to cast converging beams on the water beneath us to establish our height at 60 feet. Next it was formation runs, first over Derwent Water and then Lake Windermere. After more formation flying and a streamed landing at RAF Scampton the operation really got started.'

Richard Todd recalls the arrival of the Lancasters at Scampton: 'It will never be forgotten by members of the RAF and the film company who were present that day. There was that unmistakable hum of the aircraft in the distance and then four of them, in V-formation, came in low over the airfield, a big swing turn, then they landed in formation on the grass. There wasn't a dry eye in the house.'

The weather across the British Isles in the months of June, July and August 1954 was far from ideal from the point of view of filming. On the whole, that summer was rather dull and cool, with low temperatures and a general lack of sunshine, as well as heavy rainfall in many areas. During July a large military

The twin towers of the Derwent dam in the Derbyshire Peak District doubled for the Möhne dam in filming.
Mike Cawsey/Garbett & Goulding Collection

exercise centred on Scampton was staged to simulate the outbreak of a nuclear war. Exercise Dividend restricted all flying activity by non-operational aircraft and this, together with a spell of bad weather towards the end of the month, hindered the aerial filming programme.

Eric Quinney: 'We flew most days if the weather was suitable and on quite a few when it was not. We would some-times do two hours flying and get no productive filming due either to too much cloud, the wrong sort of light, or some other technicality. The director

had no concept of how fatiguing it was flying these heavy aircraft and would expect us to fly a second sortie if the first was unsatisfactory.'

There were no power flying controls on the Lancaster so it required a high degree of physical fitness and effort on the part of the pilot to control and manoeuvre such a large aircraft, especially at low level.

Gil Taylor remembers that the poor weather was a major hindrance for the second unit crew and did nothing to facilitate the aerial camera work:

'The big trouble was with the weather: it was the worst summer for years. The planes were full of petrol and so we just couldn't sit and wait and hope for the weather to improve. We flew over the whole of southern England and up beyond Manchester to chase the clear weather. We simply couldn't get the sun we needed, so on at least one occasion we literally chased the sun over to Holland – in fact to wherever we could get some exposure for matching weather. It was the biggest problem of all.'

Now, that is low: Lancaster NX782 is flown along the Derwent reservoir leading to the Derwent dam.
Canal Plus Screengrab

(Opposite) The sheer exhilaration of low-level flying can only be guessed at in this evocative shot of one of the Lancasters chasing the Wellington camera plane across the English countryside. The proximity of the house in the foreground gives an idea of just how low they were flying.
Mike Cawsey/Garbett & Goulding Collection

(Opposite) Above the still waters of Lake Windermere, England's largest lake, with the Langdale Chase Hotel nestling in the trees along the shore, the distinctive sound of Roll-Royce Merlin engines disturbs the calm of the Lake District.
Mike Cawsey/Garbett & Goulding Collection

Filming them filming us: the camera Varsity holding station off the starboard wing of one of the Lancasters during filming.
Mike Cawsey/Garbett & Goulding Collection

A close call with a tower of the Derwent dam.
Via Ted Szuwalski

When it came to juggling the commercial requirements of the film company and the goodwill of the aircrew and their families, particularly when much of the filming was undertaken at weekends, it was difficult to strike the right balance. As chief pilot, Ken Souter was very mindful of the fact that a lot of the flying was undertaken during his crews' leisure time. *'I was unhappy about us flying at weekends. The boys*

Cameraman Gil Taylor and the pilot of the Varsity camera plane (probably P/Off Mathieson) share a joke with the aircraft's navigator during filming.
Canal Plus

were married and their wives were getting a bit jumpy,' he recalls. Gil Taylor was also sensitive to this problem, but the filming schedule meant that sometimes he was on the receiving end of any bad feeling engendered by the situation.

'When the weather was really bad I took the aircrews to the pub and bought them drinks. Occasionally, this didn't go down well with their wives. If the weather closed in when we were away shooting we'd divert to the nearest airfield and pick up a billet for the night. That's why the pilots' wives got angry!'

John West was a National Service sergeant air gunner with 83 Squadron at RAF Hemswell. He flew as Lancaster aircrew on several occasions for filming, but on 13 August he flew with F/Lt Ken

Souter on an aerial filming sortie that, according to his flying logbook, lasted for 3 hours and 10 minutes:

'I'd not done close formation flying before apart from for the Queen's Coronation Review flypast in July 1953. During the winter of 1953–4 we had done some low flying operationally in Lincolns over Malaya, so it wasn't altogether a novelty to me, but for the film the low-level close-formation stuff gave me a real adrenaline rush. Low flying in close formation was a bit hairy. The planes rocked from side to side in flight.

When we flew over the Derwent dam in very tight formation I was in the lead plane of three as tail-end charlie [rear gunner]. I had the best view from the tail turret and was therefore better placed to advise my pilot over the intercom where the other two aircraft were in relation to us. My skipper then radioed the other two pilots and told them to come in closer or back off.'

Pilot Ted Szuwalski recalls how on a number of occasions they flew at very low level in a three-ship formation through the Kirkstone Pass in the Lake District towards Lake Windermere. The fine-tuning of their height above the ground and positioning relative to one another in flight were controlled through a radio link with the camera plane, and a radio operator working with a ground-based camera crew who were also filming the formation, but from below. There was, of course, direct radio communication between each of the Lancaster crews.

Eric Quinney remembers that flying for the film was the most exciting time in his twenty-odd years as an RAF pilot:

'To be able to fly legally at a height of a mere 60 feet is exciting, but to do this in tight formation with some 30 tons of aircraft being controlled by one hand on the

A formation take-off, probably from the grass airfield at Kirton-in-Lindsey. The sight of three Lancasters turning on to finals at this former fighter base north of Lincoln was too much for its station commander. Fearing an accident, he eventually banned Associated British from any further filming at his airfield.

Canal Plus E54.1.PUB.156

Photographed by Mike
Cawsey from the cockpit of
Wellington T10, MF628, the
Wimpy follows the ribbon-
like road that snakes
through the Kirkstone Pass.
At 1,489 feet above sea
level, it is the highest road
pass in the Lake District.
Mike Cawsey/ Garbett
& Goulding Collection

control column and one on the throttles
really does get the adrenaline flowing.
With three Lancasters in formation, each
with a wingspan of over 100 feet, it is
impressive but quite frightening when
the lead aircraft starts to follow the
prescribed route. One's tendency is to
edge away from the lead aircraft slightly
as you feel he is going to slip down into

you, but you can't do that because in
the banked turn you are much closer to
the ground than 60 feet with your lower
wingtip.'

'Any young pilot will tell you the best
way to fly is low and fast and if it is
authorised so much the better,' says
Dickie Lambert. 'I know I enjoyed it, but
my two navigators opted out very quickly

and I had to rely on volunteers for crew.'

James Fell remembers how low they actually flew during filming: *'A fair amount of filming went on at the Derwent reservoir with the Lancasters flying between the twin towers of the dam. After one filming sortie our ground crew reported on our return that we had bits of branches and leaves attached beneath the aircraft, so evidently we had clipped a tree.'*

Passing over the parapet of the Derwent dam, photographed from the cockpit of the Varsity camera aircraft by Mike Cawsey.
Mike Cawsey/Garbett & Goulding Collection

During training for the dams raid in 1943, Henry Maudslay returned from a low-level training sortie with foliage caught in the tail wheel of his Lancaster. A similar scene is recreated here during filming with Lancaster NX782.
Canal Plus

On the real raid in 1943, the Lancasters of 617 Squadron were required to fly at a height of exactly 60 feet over the Ruhr dams to release their bouncing bombs. When this was re-created for the cameras of Associated British in 1954, 60 feet actually looked a lot higher on film when the rushes were viewed, so for much of the low level work Erwin Hillier asked Ken Souter and his team to fly a lot lower, at 40 feet. Later, on at least

one occasion, Ken flew low enough over the Derwent reservoir for the down-draught from his Lancaster's four propellers to draw up individual water-spouts. *'I had a few disagreements with Erwin Hillier,'* recalls Ken. *'He was a bit Teutonic in his manner and wanted us to go lower and I told him straight that it was too bloody dangerous. I also had arguments with the film company about this.'* But Erwin Hillier prevailed, and Ken and his team flew their Lancasters at 40 feet for much of the time during filming.

However, low-level and close formation flying was not without its dangers, as Gil Taylor remembers: *'There*

were a few occasions during filming when we came close to disaster. Flying over Lake Windermere on one sortie, I gave the signal to turn to port and the Varsity responded which meant we gained height. The Lanc closest to us turned in towards us. We saw what was happening and our pilot dropped the Varsity like a stone until we picked up a bit of greenery and lost the port wingtip light. The Lanc went over the top, only just missing us.'

The stirring sight of two Lancasters, NX679 (G) and NX673 (P), stepped-up in line astern, viewed from RT686 and captured on camera by Mike Cawsey.
Mike Cawsey/Garbett & Goulding Collection

Bob Jones (left) and George Blackwell (right) discuss shooting requirements with a member of the production team.
Canal Plus E54.1.PUB.47

No. 97 Squadron signaller Sgt Bill French recalls: *'Navigation was difficult at low level because of the lack of visible reference points, and of course the need to steer clear of spires and pylons.*

When close formation was required, the bumping up and down motions gave the impression that if we hit any air turbulence we stood a good chance of crashing into each other.'

Time carried forward :— 1225·50 / 807·00 | 418·50

Date	Hour	Aircraft Type and No.	Pilot	Duty	REMARKS (including results of bombing, gunnery, exercises, etc.)	Flying Times Day	Night
14-8-54	1250	LANC VII RT686	F/S Kmiecok	Air Engineer	"Dambusters" Low Level Formation. ·30 F.P.	2·30	
19-8-54	0935	LINC II SX925	F/O Chapple	Air Engineer	Radar X/co. 1·30 Eng Flying.	3·50	
20-8-54	1320	LINC II RFA14	F/L Chapple	Air Engineer	Air Test. Double engine change.	1·15	
20-8-54	11·10	LANC VII NX673	F/S Kmiecek	Air Engineer	Base to Scampton	0·20	
21-8-54	1645	LANC VII NX673	F/O Lambert	Air Engineer.	"Dambusters" Formation Flypast Lincoln Cathedral (Low Level).	1·30	
22-8-54	1000	VARSITY WS412	P/O Mathieson	Air Engineer	"Dambusters" Lake Windermere	2·30	
22-8-54	1530	LANC VII NX673	F/Lt Souter	Air Engineer	Scampton to Base.	0·15	
23-8-54	0930	LINC II RA665	F/O Chapple	Air Engineer	Radar Runs		2·45
24-8-54	0910	LINC II RF460	F/O Chapple	Air Engineer	Base to Mildenhall	1·00	
24-8-54			—	—	Mildenhall to Base. Radar Runs. ·25 F.P.	2·05	
26-8-54	1200	LANC VII NX673	F/Sgt Szuwalski	Air Engineer	Grass Take Offs.	0·30	
26-8-54	1300	—"	—	—	"Dambusters" Formation.	0·40	

TOTAL TIME ... 826·10 | 413·55
1245·00

Thus, with the perils of low flying ever present in the minds of the men who flew the Lancasters, James Fell says they did ask Associated British what would happen if a Lancaster was to crash during filming. 'They said they would cancel the film.'

Scenes that recreate 617 Squadron's training flights in England and Wales before Operation 'Chastise' (the code-

Mike Cawsey's log book records the sorties he flew over a period in August 1954. Interspersed with his Lancaster flying for the film are four Lincoln sorties, showing that the serious business of operational flying was still ongoing.
Mike Cawsey

name for the dams raid) and the actual operations over the Ruhr dams themselves, were filmed over and along Lake Windermere in the Lake District and the Derwent dam and reservoir in the Derbyshire Peak District. Ken Souter describes something of what was required on camera: *'Windermere was quite simple to fly along, but flying across the lake was a different matter altogether. We had to come down a* *slope then flatten out across the lake and climb up over a mountain on the other side. This was quite hairy because there was not enough power to get up over the other side. I do recall that we got quite a bit of flak from the yachting fraternity on Windermere for our low flying, though! Derwent was just a swoop down between the two towers and not as prolonged as Windermere.'*

The Langdale Chase Hotel in its stunning lakeside setting between Windermere and Ambleside, was 'bombed' with toilet rolls by one of the Lancasters during filming. Derek Browne, who was camera operator to Erwin Hillier, recalls the occasion: 'As the shooting schedule was very tight, Erwin briefed and trusted me to go up in a Lancaster to shoot some of the low flying footage. With the exuberance of youth I could not resist the temptation to drop a few objects, i.e. toilet rolls, out of the bomb doors over Lake Windermere. Erwin knew nothing of this until he received a memo from the production office. Apparently, one of the displaced crowned heads of Europe was staying in a hotel that received a "direct hit". The king was not amused and I received a bollocking from Erwin.'
Mike Cawsey/Garbett & Goulding Collection

(Opposite) Gil Taylor, cameraman, Val Stewart, operator, and Tony White, assistant, at work in the Varsity camera plane.
Canal Plus

A fine study of Lancasters NX679 (G) and NX673 (P) over the Lincolnshire countryside during filming.
Mike Cawsey/Garbett & Goulding Collection

The special requirements of low-level flying meant that the pilots and their flight engineers needed to work very closely together, as Mike Cawsey recalls: *'We simulated a delivery scene at Scampton on the morning of 7 May, with a low formation flypast and circuit. It was on this occasion that I learned I had to be a mind reader as well as an engineer. Ted was busy pumping the throttles as we climbed away between the hangars but we were not holding station. I reminded Ted we only had about 2,400rpm and got the answer* "Why haven't you given me more?" *I set 2,850 and we got back on to station.'*

For Ken Souter, the most difficult part of the filming was when he had to fly through the probing fingers of the searchlight beams as the Lancasters cross the 'Dutch' coast: *'They put dimmers on the searchlights to lessen the glare for us, but they had to take them off again later for the cameras. Flying into such very bright lights made it very dangerous for us. Group Captain Whitworth said he wouldn't sanction it, and if we did it then it was at our own* risk. *We did it and got congratulatory telegrams after these shots!'*

Dickie Lambert experienced a different kind of problem during the filming of the searchlight scene: *'I must have been very close behind the Varsity because my windscreen became covered in oil. Below me was Langham airfield. I decided to land (at night and no lights), quickly clean the windscreen and then rejoin the unit in the air. No problem to me but I believe the locals thought the war had restarted and I also understand it upset a couple of poachers.'*

Dick's signaller, Sgt Bill French, recalls: *'It was about 2015hrs when suddenly there was one hell of a burst of blinding light from the searchlights and the Lancasters and camera aircraft split up and went their own way in great haste. To make matters worse, Dick Lambert could not see a damn thing because the windscreen was completely smeared in some sort of gunge. Things got rather hairy when there we were, late in the evening with almost zero visibility, nowhere near any airfield to give Dick my assistance in landing the aircraft. In the end he decided to land at Langham to clear up the mess.'*

A fair amount of flying activity for the film was conducted from the grass airfield at RAF Kirton-in-Lindsey, a former Fighter Command base 16 miles north of Lincoln. At the time of the dams raid in May 1943, Scampton was still a grass airfield. It had its concrete runways laid not long afterwards. For reasons of authenticity, it is probable that Kirton was used for filming because its grass runway resembled wartime Scampton. In 1954, Kirton was no longer an operational airfield and hosted No. 1 Initial Training School equipped with Tiger Moths for basic training of aircrew officers. Mike Cawsey remembers that the most exciting occasion was his first visit to the airfield on 26 May:

'We were briefed to fly a circuit in formation and then land – still in formation. The landing was not a problem in itself and we were all down and rolling towards the north-west corner of the airfield in a neat gaggle. The grass was wet and retardation was not particularly good. By now, all of the aircraft were trying hard to stop before the perimeter was reached but the Kirton groundcrew had picked out an aircraft each and were trying to marshal them to the

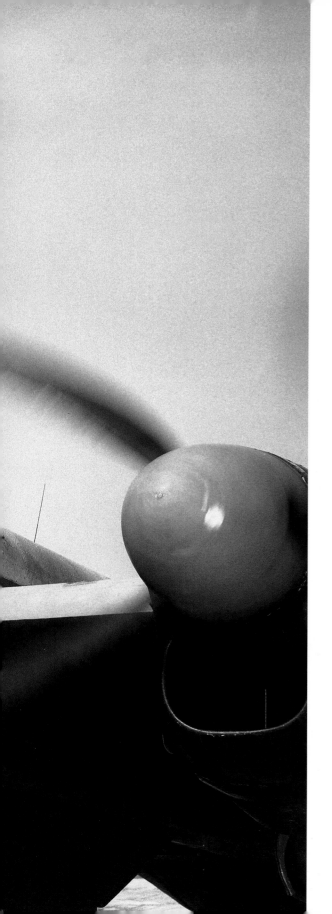

positions required by the film crew. And we were busy trying to stop without colliding with each other as the space available became narrower and the aeroplanes closer. I'm pleased to say all ended well and the aircraft were later re-positioned to suit the film crew.'

The one and only formation take-off was filmed at Kirton, and is believed to have been completed during three brief sorties in the early afternoon of 26 August. Eric Quinney recalls Joe Kmiecik telling him that following this event Kirton's station commander had withdrawn permission for any further filming of flying sequences because he was not prepared to lose the station's flight safety record.

'From the moment when the station commander saw our Lancasters turning in to land on his grass airfield he decided there and then that he didn't want us,' says Ted Szuwalski. Taking off in formation from this small airfield was fraught with potential danger, as Ken Souter remembers: 'We had to really rev up the engines, then release the brakes and take off. We could only just get off without hitting the huts at the end. The station commander wasn't

'Contact!' Under the super-vision of an RAF pilot crouching out of shot on the floor of the cockpit, Richard Todd starts up the engines of his Lancaster.
Canal Plus E54.1.PROD.42

the aerial filming

Lancasters RT686 (M) and
NX679 (G) in close forma-
tion at low level over the
outskirts of Lincoln.
Mike Cawsey/Garbett &
Goulding Collection

Lancasters taxi out from their dispersal pans at RAF Hemswell.
Canal Plus

very happy and said we had to leave.' James Fell, who was the air signaller in Joe Kmiecik's crew, remembers further details of the circumstances that led to this ban:

'The director wanted to film an aircraft flying at the control tower on take-off. This was not possible at Scampton due to the configuration of the runways, so we flew up to Kirton-in-Lindsey where this could be done. After due deliberation, Joe Kmiecik took off towards the control tower and hangars for what was thought to be a good shot, complete with cumulus clouds in the background. Joe's Lanc narrowly missed the tower and the hangar. His

wife who was watching was so upset that she walked off the station in a state of shock. The station commander thought the whole thing was too dangerous and grounded us, banning the Lancasters from any further flying from his airfield. Later, he allowed us one trip out to return to Scampton and told us never to return.

'We went back to Hemswell and used the grassy area in between the runways,' recalls Ted, 'but it wasn't smooth enough. On one occasion we hit a bump on our take-off run which made the Lanc suddenly get airborne, but we were practically at stalling speed and I really struggled to keep her in the air.'

For the purposes of the film, actor Richard Todd had to be seen starting up and taxying a Lancaster. On occasions he actually piloted a Lanc on its take-off run at speeds of up to 70mph. *'To give Richard Todd and the actor who played the part of his flight engineer [Robert Shaw] their due,'* recalls pilot Eric Quinney, *'they learned the start-up sequence to perfection and carried out this procedure themselves while an RAF engineer supervised them from beneath on the cockpit floor.'*

Ted Szuwalski remembers the occasion on which he helped Richard Todd with the engine start-up sequence: *'In the scene where Richard Todd is starting up the engines of his Lancaster before setting out on the raid, it was actually me who started up the Lanc from the right-hand seat with Todd sitting in the left-hand seat. He was holding his hand up to the ground engineer shouting "Number one!*

Lancaster NX673 (P) in her element above the craggy landscape of the Lake District.
Mike Cawsey/Garbett & Goulding Collection

Richard Todd and Robert Shaw run through cockpit checks prior to engine start-up, a procedure that they mastered to perfection during filming.
Canal Plus E54.1.PUB.149

Number two!" etcetera out of the cock-pit window. I had to be out of sight of the camera so I needed to be down on the cockpit floor to start the engines.'

Once he had made his take-off run

for the camera, sadly for Todd he then had to throttle back the engines and return the Lancaster to the dispersal point. The start-up and taxying scenes were all shot at Hemswell.

AERIAL FILMING

April 1954 was a busy month for the Lancaster crews with familiarisation flights followed by the first filming sorties. May was less busy, and the months of June and July were relatively unproductive where it concerned aerial filming involving the Lancasters. August and September each saw close to twenty hours of air-to-air film work, while the most intensive activity took place on 4 September, when almost six hours filming of low-level formation flying was achieved over Lake Windermere.

Scenes showing early tests of the bouncing bomb at Reculver were shot off the shoreline at Skegness in Lincolnshire because it was near to the main filming activity at Hemswell and Scampton. The practice flights before the raid, and the actual bombing runs over the dams during the raid itself, were filmed mainly along Lake Windermere and through the Kirkstone Pass in the Lake District, and at the Derwent reservoir and dam in the Derbyshire Peak District. (The latter was one of three dams actually used by 617 Squadron in April and May 1943 for intensive flying training before the raid.) For additional low-level filming in the Lake District over Windermere, the Lancasters and second unit crew were detached to RAF Silloth in Cumbria at the end of August for a week.

The flight to the dams over the Dutch lowlands was simulated over the dead flat fenlands between Boston in Lincolnshire and King's Lynn, just across the Great Ouse in Norfolk. Scenes of the Lancasters crossing the 'enemy coast' were shot over Gibraltar Point near Skegness, or along the coast near Southwold in Suffolk. However, Eric Quinney also remembers the 'enemy coast' as being the west coast of Anglesey in North Wales, which he over flew in 'P' for Popsie.

For what must be obvious reasons, the RAF and Associated British were unable to secure permission to film the raid sequences over the actual Ruhr dams themselves, so much use was made of studio models and the Derwent dam for filming.

The scenes of inundation in the Ruhr valley that appear towards the end of the film were photographed in 1954 when the area of the dams itself fell victim to a natural flood disaster. Michael Anderson sent a film unit to Germany specially to capture this event for incorporation in the final version of the film.

Lincoln Cathedral photographed by Mike Cawsey from Lancaster NX673, piloted by F/Off Dick Lambert, on 21 August 1954.
Mike Cawsey/Garbett & Goulding Collection

The pressures of low flying to a tight brief from the director meant that when the business of the day had been completed, the crews would adjourn to a local hostelry to unwind with a well-earned drink.

'At the end of each day we would meet at the Saracen's Head Hotel on

the High Street in Lincoln, a well-known watering hole for Bomber Command crews,' recalls Jim Fell. 'It was run by the Levine family who also owned the White Hart near Lincoln Cathedral. In a practice that was common in hotels in the fifties they provided their customers with pint tankards, not quite silver but

Elkington plate. Apparently, Guy Gibson used to call the most popular bar at the Saracen's the "Snake Pit". I wonder why!'

Pilot Ted Szuwalski also remembers how they would meet for a drink at the Saracen's Head and wait for the film to finish at the Savoy cinema in Saltergate before walking over to watch the rushes of the day's location filming. *'The reason for this was that if some of the flying was not to the director's liking, then he could explain what he wanted much more easily with the film on the screen in front of us,'* explains Ted. *'Of course, we did have some formal pre-flight briefings but most of the film people had little experience of aerial filming and we RAF crews had no experience of flying for films, especially at low level and in formation. Hopefully, by seeing the rushes, we could correct any problems with the flying in our next sortie.'*

On one such night after watching the rushes, some of the aircrews returned to the Saracen's with the director and a few of the production team for a late drink. Jim Fell remembers what happened. *'The barmaid who ran the "Snake Pit" did so in a military fashion and stood for no hanky panky whatsoever: cross her and you would go thirsty. If you were in her good books you were duty bound to listen to one of her risqué jokes. A very senior member of the production team made a severe error of judgement and made a pass at her. He not only got a flea in his ear but also a bump on the head for his trouble. He couldn't believe it!'*

When the location work was completed in September, the RAF aircrews that had flown the Lancasters, Wellington and Varsity aircraft on camera, together with the second unit crew, were treated to a slap-up lunch at a hotel in Lincoln, hosted by Michael Anderson and Bill Whittaker. There were many more receptions and parties given at the time to thank those who had been involved in making *The Dam Busters*.

The Air Officer Commanding, 1 Group, Air Vice-Marshal John Whitley, was delighted with the film and the tremendous public relations job it had done for the RAF. In a letter to Gp Capt Dudley Burnside, the Officer Commanding RAF Hemswell, he thanked all those RAF personnel who had taken part in the filming, and in particular Ken Souter, Dickie Lambert,

Joe Kmiecik and Ted Szuwalski for their special contribution:

'All of us in 1 Group must feel immensely proud that Hemswell, Lindholme and Scampton's contribution has been a greater factor than any towards its [the film's] success . . . I know that this meant a great deal of spare time being sacrificed last summer by both air and ground crews, and that their only reward could be that they were taking part in a picture which might possibly do much to enhance the prestige of the RAF. That this will have been the result of all their good work is now beyond a shadow of a doubt.'

The last word on the contribution made to the film by the RAF pilots must go to Richard Todd who says, *'those RAF chaps in the film took a lot of chances and did a wonderful, wonderful job for us'*.

When the location filming came to an end, it was a huge anti-climax to the crews who had been flying the Lancasters for the past six months. It also marked a change of role for 83 and 97 Squadrons, from front-line bomber squadrons to training units. Both of the squadrons now became involved with training navigators for the new V-force – the era of the piston-engine bomber had reached an end and the dawn of the jet bomber age had finally arrived. In December 1955, both squadrons departed RAF Hemswell with 83 moving to nearby RAF Waddington where it dropped its number identity and was renamed Antler Squadron. It was re-formed in May 1957 as 83 Squadron and subsequently became the first squadron in Bomber Command to be equipped with the Avro Vulcan. No. 97 Squadron was renamed Arrow Squadron in January 1956 and later re-formed at RAF Hemswell as a Thor Inter-continental Ballistic Missile squadron in December 1958. For this famous bomber squadron the transition from manned aircraft to unmanned missile marked the end of an illustrious career spanning 40 years.

6 main filming and post-production

> The film took about ten months from start of model shooting to seeing the first print from the lab. It was a tightly scripted film and ABPC were not the sort of company to waste money on over-shooting.
>
> Richard Best, *Editor*, **The Dam Busters**

he Dam Busters was a joy to edit and one lived the whole drama of the story,' says Richard Best, who was responsible for editing many hours of continuous film into 120 minutes of box office success. It was a technically complex film, but careful forward planning by Associated British had made available some of the best technical and artistic brains in the business, notably Erwin Hillier as Director of Photography, Gilbert Taylor as Director of Special Effects Photography, Robert Jones as Art Director, and Richard Best as Editor.

'From my point of view as Director,' says Michael Anderson, *'my job was to choose a team that was skilled, had vision, and would work closely in harmony together.'*

As we have seen in Chapter 5, the flying was mostly out of RAF Hemswell, with the aerial sequences filmed over eastern England and the north-west. Many of the squadron and domestic sequences were staged at RAF Scampton where main unit filming began in April 1954. Camera crews also filmed at a number of other locations in

Richard Todd and G/Capt J.N.H. Whitworth on set during a break from filming. Whitworth, who had been the station commander of RAF Scampton at the time of the dams raid, was asked to act as a technical adviser to the film company in 1954.

'Charles' Whitworth was a brave and highly experienced bomber pilot who had flown operationally since the beginning of the Second World War. As a squadron leader he had been awarded the DFC in May 1940, with a bar to the award later in the year, and the DSO in 1941. Until his appointment to command Scampton, his service had been exclusively with the Yorkshire-based 4 Group. He had flown over Germany, France, Norway, Italy and Czechoslovakia with 10 Squadron (Whitleys), 78 Squadron (Whitleys and Halifaxes), and 35 Squadron (Halifaxes), the last two of which he commanded.
Canal Plus E54.1.PUB.102

(Opposite) The 640-ft ship tank No. 2 at the National Physical Laboratory, Teddington, was used by Barnes Wallis for some of the original feasibility tests for the bouncing bomb. It was revisited by the film crew during the making of *The Dam Busters*. In 1998 the tank and the building in which it was housed was swept aside to make way for a car park.
Canal Plus ES4.1.PUB.33

RAF Scampton was the backdrop for much of the location filming, with the sergeants' mess (pictured) used by Associated British to represent the briefing room for the crews prior to the dams raid.

England that included the National Physical Laboratory at Teddington, and the Building Research Station at Garston, near Watford – both of which were the locations for the original tests connected with the dams raid. In

addition to the four Lancaster aircraft that were taken out of storage specially for the film, eleven vehicles were borrowed from the Ministry of Supply disposal dump at Scampton for use on the set. RAF personnel at both

The 5 Group operations room was accurately re-created for the film from photographs and plans of the original building. From left to right: Basil Sydney ('Bomber' Harris), Michael Redgrave (Wallis), Derek Farr (Whitworth) and Ernest Clark (Cochrane).
Canal Plus

Hemswell and Scampton were also loaned as extras for certain scenes in the film.

At Elstree, the set builders and model makers re-created office interiors for Bomber Harris, Gibson and Wallis, as well as a number of room interiors at RAF Scampton, and the 5 Group operations room. Although the 5 Group's real underground operations room at Grantham had been sealed up at the end of the war, by a stroke of luck it had remained untouched since then, its contents frozen in time. Associated British had discovered this fact and were allowed inside to photograph this remarkable time capsule, thereby enabling them to re-create a faithful studio mock-up for the film.

The visual impact of the film was very

At Elstree, three huge models of the Ruhr dams were built on a sound stage. This is the Möhne, lit for night and shown at the point when it was 'breached' for the camera.
Canal Plus E54.1.PROD.147

reliant on the ability of the special effects people to simulate the explosions of the bouncing bombs and the dam walls crumbling away under the massive back-pressure of water. Therefore, three enormous authentic scale mock-ups of

the dams, their lakes and surrounding countryside were created at Elstree Studios. They measured 300 feet long by 150 feet wide, and filled an entire sound stage. There was just enough room to manoeuvre a camera crane

Most of the film was shot in broad daylight with the clever use of coloured filters to simulate darkness. The low flying was real enough, though, at 40 feet above the surface of the water.
Canal Plus Screengrab

Similar technical wizardry was needed to create this montage of Gibson's bomb-aimer, 'Spam' Spafford (Nigel Stock), about to release the first bouncing bomb over the Möhne lake.
Canal Plus E54.1.PROD.196

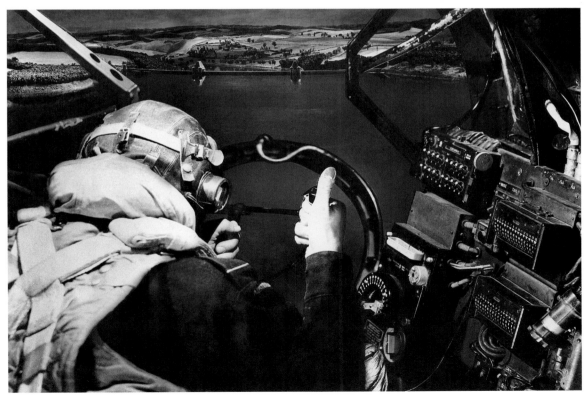

Tracer bullets and flak were matted on to a shot of the dam by a contract special effects company in Soho.
Canal Plus E54.1.PROD.151

around the sides. Camera tracks and a swinging arm for the high-speed camera were also added to facilitate filming. The model set was lit for night and to simulate the appearance of water on a real lake, twenty-eight giant fans, each adjusted to a different speed, were positioned around the set to cause ripples on the surface of the water. Apart from the general views of the dams and surrounding countryside, most of these

shots were used as viewpoints from inside the Lancasters or as back-projection for these scenes. The enormous explosion as the Möhne dam is finally breached was 'matted' on to the long-shot of the dam by a contract special effects company in Soho, which also added the tracer bullets and flak.

For the scenes depicting action inside the Lancasters themselves, Associated British constructed mock-

Waiting for the moment when they join the transports to take them out to the dispersals and their waiting aircraft, actors and RAF personnel extras mingle together on the grass at Scampton.
Canal Plus E54.1.PROD.38

The pre-take-off cockpit checks and start-up procedures for the Lancaster were fairly complicated affairs, but Richard Todd and Robert Shaw mastered them under the tutelage of an RAF engineer and supervised on set by an RAF pilot.
Canal Plus E54.1.PROD.29

ups of the various crew stations, as well as installing a complete Lancaster nose section in the studio, mounted on a pivoting platform. Head of special effects photography, Gil Taylor (who had also been the cameraman on many J. Lee Thompson films), recalls: *'Harold Payne devised the machinery that replicated the movements of an aircraft in flight for filming in the studio. He really was a most respected man in the camera department.'* The cockpit controls were linked to a motor beneath the platform to create what was in essence a simple flight simulator. When the control column was moved the platform moved too, thereby creating a realistic flying movement of the aircraft nose section when eventually viewed on screen.

During the long spells of filming in the studio, Richard Todd was strapped into the pilot's seat in the nose section for hours at a time while scenes were shot and shot again until the director was happy with the result. To help pass the time in between 'takes', Todd was taught how to 'fly' the platform correctly by an RAF flying instructor. He learned how to operate a Lancaster up to take-off speed. For the purposes of the film

You can almost hear the four Merlins champing at the bit and the hiss of compressed air from the brakes, as a film Lancaster taxies around the peri track at Hemswell. Note the crew ladder being pulled up into the hatch beneath the cockpit. In the background can be seen the squat form of Wellington T10, MF628.

Canal Plus E54.1.PUB.110

when on location, he had to be seen starting up and taxying and on occasions he actually piloted a Lancaster on its take-off run at speeds of up to 70mph. *'I did get up to take-off speed during the taxying scenes,'* says Richard Todd, *'but I'd have loved to have gone that little extra distance!'*

Pilot Eric Quinney recalls: *'To give Richard Todd and the actor who played the part of his flight engineer [Robert Shaw] their due, they learned the start-up sequence to perfection and carried out this procedure themselves while an RAF engineer supervised from the floor of the cockpit.'*

All the filming was completed by late September. The picture was finally 'in the can' now and post-production work could begin. Nearly a year was to pass before the première, and another three months before the film's general release on 5 September 1955. By a happy coincidence, Michael Anderson's next film assignment was at Elstree, so this interval allowed him to become thoroughly involved and take a more active role in the post-production phase than would usually have been the case.

It was at this point that the post-production team at Elstree became involved. Headed by Arthur Southgate, they dealt with sound effects, including the 're-voicing' of actors where the location sound was not up to standard. By the end of shooting Richard Best, the film editor, had edited the whole film together and showed it to Michael Anderson, Bill Whittaker and others. 'From memory, few alterations were made,' says Best. There was a showing for Leighton Lucas to determine the places where music was required, and the theme and incidental music was then recorded. These music tracks were fitted to the film by the editor. The individual sound tracks were balanced and mixed down on to one track in dubbing sessions to become the soundtrack on the married print from the lab. Then the negative was cut at the lab to match the work print and a first married print delivered. But this is an over-simplification of the post-production process that does not do full justice to what is a complex and highly professional business.

In a fine example of the painstaking attention to detail involved in the post-

production phase, to create the single close-up shot of Gibson in flight over the Möhne dam, looking out of the cockpit window of his Lancaster, while flak zips past and another Lancaster passes beneath, it was necessary to shoot six separate 'travelling matts': a studio shot of Todd in the mock-up Lancaster cockpit, the model of the dam, photographed flak, the landscape background to the model dam, an explosion (featuring a different model), and a Lancaster in flight. Each matt had to be photographed at precisely the right angle of vision, and each had to be in correct proportion to its size when viewed from that distance.

As the film's editor, Richard Best had a key role to play in *The Dam Busters*. His artistic interpretation of the many miles of film, shot on location and in the studio at great expense in terms of both time and money, could make or break the production.

'*The film took about ten months from start of model shooting to seeing the first print from the lab. The running time is two hours and I am sure the first cut was not a great deal over. It was a tightly scripted film and ABPC were not the sort of company to waste money on over-*

Deceiving the eye: it took six separate shots overlaid one on top of the other to achieve this dramatic image of Guy Gibson (Richard Todd) watching from his Lancaster cockpit as the flood waters gush out of the Möhne dam.
Canal Plus E54.1.PROD.165

shooting and leave, say, 45 minutes on the cutting room floor. No sequences were removed, so tightening up was the main concern.

'A film is not viable without editing, One has to have a "dramatic" sense in order to feel the emotion and logic of sequences. Hundreds of shots are photographed during production and one's job is to feel where to use any part

Gibson (Richard Todd) briefs his crews before the raid. On the table in front of him, in its protective wooden box, is the actual three-dimensional model of the Möhne dam and its lake, specially made for aircrew briefing purposes by the RAF's CIU at Medmenham in the Thames valley. Lost among the faces in the background are some of the RAF aircrews from Hemswell who flew the Lancasters on the film, and who were also extras in the crew briefing scenes.
Canal Plus

When Todd is briefing his crews, the camera angles are changed every few seconds.
Canal Plus E54.1.PROD.128

or parts of each shot at any one time. The film has to be dramatically constructed from the material seen in the rushes, and hopefully interpreting the director's intentions. All the elements are there but they have to be mined.

'Watch any film and note the change of angle, every few seconds perhaps, but never for very long: long shots, medium shots, over-shoulder close shots, single close shots, all following each other quite quickly at times. For example, when Todd is briefing his crews, watch how many times the angles are changed and the various pieces showing men listening are seen. This is what the editor and director decided was the best construction to make the point. Hours and hours of rushes, every shot at full length with clapperboard and the director calling "action!" and "cut!" would be quite useless on their own.

With the distinctive crackle of its four Merlins reined back after hours of full throttle flying, a film Lancaster taxies past the camera as another Lanc, its wing flaps set at 25° and its propellers set fully fine, comes in to land.
On the ground can also be seen a Station Flight Airspeed Oxford, and de Havilland Mosquito PR35, VR803. In the background is the distinctive checkered flare path caravan that was a common feature on wartime RAF bomber airfields.
Canal Plus E54.1.PUB.111

Richard Todd explains a point of interest to Michael Redgrave and one of the production team during location shooting on the Lincolnshire coast.
Canal Plus E54.1.PUB.128

'Luckily, in those days one could edit without interference during the shooting period. One edited the sequences as soon as possible after they were shot and so gradually built up the film. All the model shots were filmed in the first three months of 1954 and I had them put in script order so that when it came to the shots of action in the planes I could quickly find the relevant points of view.

'Fifty-six men. If I'd known it was going to be like this, I'd never have started it,' says Wallis (Michael Redgrave) to Gibson (Richard Todd). R.C. Sherriff's script, combined with Michael Anderson's directing and the masterly understated acting from Redgrave and Todd, combine to create one of the most powerful moments in the film.
Canal Plus E54.1.PROD.39

Usually, I had a copy completed about three days after shooting finished. Then we had runnings for the director and producer. Notes were taken of their comments and these were done and the edit was viewed again until all concerned were happy.

'One place in the film I thought they might want shorter was the landing of the planes after the raid. I played it long, showing almost the full entry into the frame with the wings passing over the top. This seemed to add weight to the drama and also, even, gave a feeling of weariness. I was never asked to shorten these scenes by Micky Anderson, Bill Whittaker or Robert Clark.'

In the last scene of the film, Wallis asks Gibson about the Squadron's losses on the raid. It concludes with the short but poignant line from Gibson: 'I have to write some letters first.' This is a masterly piece of acting, direction and editing. Richard Best remarks: 'Redgrave and Todd gauged it with great sensitivity, obviously with direction from Micky Anderson and great writing and dialogue from R.C. Sherriff. This scene is a prime example of how the editor can walk in the footsteps of the

actors and director and feel the emotions they have engendered and edit accordingly, giving the right emphasis to each actor. And also, not to be afraid to let Todd walk quite a distance away before fading out.'

Richard Todd nominated this scene as his high point of the film. 'In the very last shot of all Gibson says "I've got some letters to write", and you get this little figure walking away into the distance. It's so understated, with no histrionics or heroic gestures – just this little chap walking into the distance.'

This is how it finally looked on film, but the scene – and possibly the film – could have been a lot different, as one of the Lancaster aircrew, Sgt Jim Fell, recalls:

'When Michael Redgrave was asking Richard Todd about the casualties on the raid, we got into trouble with the electricians' union. A floodlight needed moving and when one of our boys, ever helpful, unwittingly moved it, all hell was let loose. There was nearly a union walk-out, which was only prevented by grovelling apologies from us, and a lecture on the principles of the closed shop from the union steward.'

(Opposite) The lonely road of command. 'I have some letters to write…' says Gibson (Richard Todd) before walking to his office on the morning after the raid.
In reality, it was the squadron's adjutant, F/Lt Harry Humphries, assisted by the orderly room sergeant, Sgt Heveron, who sent telegrams on the morning after the raid to the next of kin of the 56 men killed or missing. Formal letters were written by Humphries over the next few days and were later 'topped and tailed' by Gibson.
Canal Plus E54.1.PROD.57

(Opposite) The trade union closed shop agreement nearly caused a walk-out on set when well-meaning RAF personnel lent a hand to move some lighting rigs.
Canal Plus

Richard Todd and his wife are caught by the photographer on première night.
Canal Plus E54.1.DBP.69

Demand for tickets to see the première of *The Dam Busters* was so great that two Royal Command performances were held in London at the Empire cinema, Leicester Square. The first showing was on 16 May 1955, the twelfth anniversary of the raid, and was attended by Princess Margaret. Also present were some of the surviving aircrew from the dams raid that included Mick Martin (skipper AJ-P), Harold Hobday (navigator AJ-N) and Bert Foxlee (front gunner AJ-P), as well as Guy Gibson's father, and his widow, Eve. The second performance on the following night was screened in the presence of the Duke and Duchess of Gloucester.

Associated British did not forget the RAF personnel, because they too had their own première of the film when a special preview was shown in the station cinema at Scampton on 20 May. Everyone from Hemswell and

Their names in lights: the frontage of the Empire in London's Leicester Square on the film's première night, 16 May 1955.
Canal Plus E54.1.DBP.79

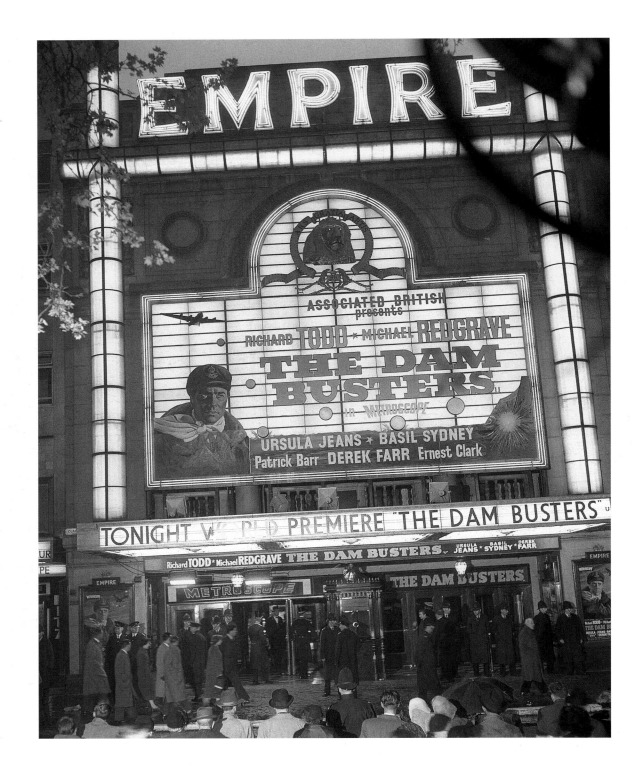

At a reception to mark the première of the film, some of the people who had made it all possible enjoy a joke and a chat. From left to right: G/Capt 'Charles' Whitworth, Paul Brickhill, Sir Barnes and Lady Wallis, Sir Philip Warter (Chairman, Associated British Picture Corporation) and Lady Warter.

Canal Plus E54.1.DBP.22

Erwin Hillier was noted for his high contrast chiaroscuro-style of black and white photography and a penchant for unusual composition. Always immaculately dressed, he would never tolerate sloppiness in any form. Erwin is pictured here on the set of *The Dam Busters* at RAF Scampton.
Canal Plus

Scampton who had been involved in making the film was invited.

On completion of the filming, Ted Szuwalksi and Ken Souter were posted to the Far East. In the early evening of 26 August 1955, they both met up again at the Shaw Theatrette in Robinson Road, Singapore City, for the Far East press preview of *The Dam Busters*.

In the fifty years that have followed its cinema release, *The Dam Busters* has been shown countless times on British television (the first time was on BBC1 in 1971). It has also been made available on video and as a DVD. In 2005 it was voted one of the all-time top war films in Channel 4's *100 Greatest War Films*, bringing the dam busters story to an even wider audience. It is now firmly established in the popular consciousness as one of the best-known war films of all time.

ERWIN HILLIER (1911–2005)

German-born cinematographer Erwin Hillier trained at Germany's UFA Studios before moving to England at the age of 18 to escape from the turmoil of Weimar Germany. He was to become one of the most important and sought-after cinematographers of the 1940s and '50s. During the Second World War he made a number of documentaries for the Ministry of Information, but it was his association with the famous Powell and Pressburger film-making partnership that put him on the map as a cinematographer. His camera work on *A Canterbury Tale* (1944) is among his finest achievements, but Hillier moved to Associated British soon afterwards where his best-known project of the '50s was *The Dam Busters*.

RICHARD BEST (1916–2004)

Richard Best had a burning passion to be in film from childhood. Born in 1916, he went into the film business in 1935 at Elstree Studios with British and Dominion as a cutting-room assistant. As his experience grew, he moved to Pinewood Studios in 1936 and then to Denham in 1938. When war broke out in 1939 he was called up and joined the Royal Berkshire Regiment, but after 18 months he applied to join the fledgling Army Film Unit. He was now a sergeant and an editor, but had never edited anything on his own before. Thrown in at the deep end, his experience and reputation swiftly grew and by the war's end he had edited a string of official documentaries that included the acclaimed *Desert Victory* (1943) and *Burma Victory* (1945), working with Captain Roy Boulting (of the famous Boulting Brothers film partnership). Not until after the war did Richard edit his first feature film, *Fame is the Spur*, starring Michael Redgrave and Rosamund John, directed by Roy Boulting. In a highly successful career that spanned 43 years, Richard edited 42 feature films including the classic desert war picture *Ice Cold in Alex* and of course *The Dam Busters*. His final film was *Dominique* (1978) with Cliff Robertson, Jenny Agutter and Jean Simmons.

Richard Best at work at the Movieola in the early 1960s.
Richard Best

Gilbert Taylor (far right) pictured at work in the Varsity camera aircraft during the making of *The Dam Busters*. His wartime experience as an aerial cameraman with the RAF Film Production Unit was an invaluable training for the air-to-air camera work required for *The Dam Busters*.
Canal Plus

GILBERT TAYLOR (b. 1914)

Head of Special Effects Photography was Gilbert Taylor who began his film career as an assistant in the Gaumont-British camera department in 1929. Gil was a founder member of the RAF's Film Production Unit (FPU) during the Second World War and as a sergeant he had been on the RAF's course for movie film in 1942. He later became the first FPU cameraman to fly operationally with Bomber Command, shooting hard-hitting cine film of the RAF's devastating night raids on German cities. Once again, it was an example of how an individual's personal war experience was to inform the interpretation of the dam busters' story. Gil was destined for great things in the film world and went on to achieve world-wide recognition and fame for his special effects photography. *Star Wars* is probably his best-known film.

ERIC COATES (1886–1957)

There are some films that are particularly memorable for their distinctive title music and *The Dam Busters* is one such picture. It is probably fair to say that its rousing 'Dam Buster March' has become one of the best-known pieces of film music ever written. When the popular composer Eric Coates was approached to write the title theme, he replied, 'I think I finished it yesterday'. In fact, he had written a suitable work some ten years earlier to mark the wartime British victory at El Alamein, but it had remained unpublished. It made the Top Ten in 1955, remained there for more than a year and has even been arranged as a hymn tune. The composer of stirring marches, bright orchestrations and pop-ular melodies, Coates became famous literally overnight for his 'Knightsbridge March', but he will be remembered by 21st-century audiences for one of his best-loved tunes, 'By the Sleepy Lagoon', better known as the theme music for BBC Radio 4's long-running musical request programme *Desert Island Discs*. By coincidence, Coates's home town of Hucknall in Nottinghamshire was where much of the wartime development work was carried out on the Rolls-Royce Merlin engine that powered the Avro Lancaster bomber.

Eric Coates, composer of the 'Dam Buster March', was dubbed the 'uncrowned king of light music' by the BBC.
Harry Smith

bibliography

1. primary sources

a: the met office
Supplement to the Daily Weather Report of the Meteorological Office, London,
July and August 1954

b: the national archives, kew (public record office)
Air 27/2638 – 97 Squadron ORB, January–December 1954

Air 28/1211 – RAF Hemswell ORB, January 1952–December 1954

Air 28/1309 – RAF Scampton ORB, December 1952–December 1961

Air 28/1271 – RAF Scampton, ORB Appendices, January 1953–August 1954

2. secondary sources

a: books
Brickhill, Paul, **The Dam Busters** (London, Evans, 1951)

Falconer, Jonathan, **RAF Bomber Command in Fact, Film and Fiction** (Stroud, Sutton Publishing, 1996)

Falconer, Jonathan, **The Dam Busters** (Stroud, Sutton Publishing, 2003)

Garbett, Mike, and Goulding, Brian, **Aircam Aviation Series No. 12: Avro Lancaster in Unit Service**
(Canterbury, Osprey Publications, 1970)

Garbett, Mike, and Goulding, Brian, **Lincoln at War 1944-1966** (Shepperton, Ian Allan, 1979, repr. 2001)

Garbett, Mike, and Goulding, Brian, **Lancaster at War: 5** (Shepperton, Ian Allan, 1995)

Humphries, Harry, **Living With Heroes: The Dam Busters** (Norwich, The Erskine Press, 2003)

Ramsden, John, **The Dam Busters: A British Film Guide** (London, I.B. Tauris, 2003)

b: newspapers

Paul Brickhill – Obituaries

Daily Telegraph, 26 April 1991

The Times, 26 April 1991

Guardian, 27 April 1991

Independent, 29 April 1991

Nigel Stock – Obituary

The Times, 24 June 1986

Group Captain J.N.H. Whitworth – Obituary

The Times, 17 November 1974

c: internet

<http://www.eh.net/hmit/>   How Much is That Worth Today?

<http://www.screenonline.org.uk/> British Film Institute Screenonline –
                                    the definitive guide to Britain's film and TV history

appendix 1
the credits

The Dam Busters
Length 11,230ft (3,423m), Cert 'U'

the cast

Barnes Wallis	Michael Regrave
Mrs Wallis	Ursula Jeans
Doctor	Charles Carson
Sir David Pye	Stanley van Beers
Doctor W.H. Glanville	Colin Tapley
Committee members	Frederick Leister, Eric Messiter, Laidman Brown
Official, National Physical Laboratory	Raymond Huntley
Official, Ministry of Aircraft Production	Hugh Manning
Captain Joseph (Mutt) Summers	Patrick Barr
Observers at trials	Edwin Styles, Hugh Moxey
RAF officer at trials	Anthony Shaw
Air Chief Marshal Sir Arthur Harris	Basil Sydney
Air Vice-Marshal the Hon. Ralph Cochrane	Ernest Clark
Group Captain J.N.H. Whitworth	Derek Farr
Farmer	Laurence Naismith
Group signals officer	Harold Siddons
BBC announcer	Frank Phillips

members of 617 squadron

Wg Cdr Guy Gibson	Richard Todd
His crew:	
Flt Lt R.D. Trevor-Roper	Brewster Mason
Flt Lt R.E.G. Hutchison	Anthony Doonan
Flg Off Spafford	Nigel Stock
Flt Lt A.T. Taerum	Brian Nissen
Flt Sgt J. Pulford	Robert Shaw
Plt Off G.A. Deering	Peter Assinder
Sqn Ldr H.M. Young	Richard Leech
Sqn Ldr H.E. Maudslay	Richard Thorp

Flt Lt J.V. Hopgood	*John Fraser*
Flt Lt W. Astell	*David Morell*
Flt Lt H.B. Martin	*Bill Kerr*
Flt Lt D.J.H. Maltby	*George Baker*
Flt Lt D.J. Shannon	*Ronald Wilson*
Flg Off L.G. Knight	*Denys Graham*
Flt Lt R.C. Hay	*Basil Appleby*
Flt Lt J.F. Leggo	*Tim Turner*
Flt Sgt G.E. Powell	*Ewen Solon*
Wg Cdr Gibson's batman	*Harold Goodwin*

the credits

Director in charge of production	*Robert Clark*
Based on the book by Paul Brickhill and on	
W/Cdr Gibson's own account in *Enemy Coast Ahead*	
Screenplay	*R.C. Sherriff*
Director of photography and aerial photography	*Erwin Hiller*
Art director	*Robert Jones*
Special effects photography	*Gilbert Taylor*
Production manager	*Gordon Scott*
Editor	*Richard Best*
Casting directors	*Robert Lennard, G.B. Walker*
Assistant director	*John Street*
Camera operators	*Norman Warwick and Val Stewart*
Sound recordist	*Leslie Hammond*
Dubbing editor	*Arthur Southgate*
Continuity	*Thelma Orr*
Make-up	*Stuart Freeborn*
Hairdresser	*Hilda Winifred Fox*
Technical adviser	*Group Captain J.N.H. Whitworth*
March, *'The Dam Busters'* by	*Eric Coates*
Music score by	*Leighton Lucas*
Performed by	*The Associated British Studio Orchestra*
Musical director	*Louis Levy*
Recording director (RCA Sound)	*H.V. King*
Production supervisor	*W.A. Whittaker*
Directed by	*Michael Anderson*
Made at Associated British Studios, Elstree, England	
World distribution by	*Associated British-Pathé*

appendix 2
the aircraft in the film

1. Avro Lancaster
Built in 1945 by Austin Motors, Longbridge, as B Mk 7s

NX673

Sept 1945 – Issued to 32 MU (RAF St Athan)

Nov 1945 – To 9 Squadron, RAF Waddington

Jan 1946 – To India for photo survey work

Apr 1946 – Returned to UK. Stored at 20 MU (RAF Aston Down)

Mar 1950 – To 5 MU (RAF Kemble)

Apr 1950 – Returned to 20 MU

May 1952 – Issued out for film work at RAF Upwood (*Appointment in London*)

Jul 1952 – To 20 MU

Mar 1954 – To RAF Hemswell for filming (*The Dam Busters*). Painted in the markings of F/Lt Mick Martin's AJ-P

Oct 1954 – Returned to 20 MU and declared non-effective stock

Jul 1956 – Scrapped

NX679

Jul 1945 – To 617 Squadron RAF Waddington

Oct 1945 – Issued to 32 MU

Jan 1946 – To India

May 1952 – Returned to UK and stored at 20 MU, issued out for film work at RAF Upwood (*Appointment in London*)

Jul 1952 – Returned to 20 MU

Sept 1953 – Transferred to non-effective stock

Mar 1954 – To RAF Hemswell for filming (*The Dam Busters*). Painted to represent W/C Guy Gibson's AJ-G/ED932, the only one of the four Lancasters to have its serial altered for the film

Oct 1954 – Returned to 20 MU and declared non-effective stock

Jul 1956 – Scrapped

NX782

Oct 1945 – Unspecified ground accident, Cat Ac

Mar 1946 – With Air Command South East Asia, probably with Tiger Force

May 1946 – Issued for return to UK

May 1952 – Issued out for film work at RAF Upwood (*Appointment in London*)

Jul 1952 – Held at 20 MU

Mar 1954 – To RAF Hemswell for filming (*The Dam Busters*). Retained as standard Mk 7 to represent W/Cdr Guy Gibson's aircraft ZN-G when CO of 106 Squadron

Oct 1954 – Returned to 20 MU and declared non-effective stock

Jul 1956 – Scrapped

RT686

Issued to 32 MU

Feb 1946 – To RAF Swinderby

Mar 1946 – To 15 MU (RAF Wroughton)

Sept 1953 – Transferred to non-effective stock

Mar 1954 – To RAF Hemswell for filming (*The Dam Busters*)

Oct 1954 – Issued to 20 MU and declared non-effective stock again

Jul 1956 – Scrapped

(Lancaster histories compiled by Trevor Green, with additional research by the author)

2. Vickers Wellington
Built in 1944 as a B Mk X by Vickers (Blackpool)

MF628

May 1944 – Issued to 18 MU, RAF Tinwald Downs

Mar 1948 – Converted to T10 by Boulton Paul, Wolverhampton

Apr 1949 – To No 1 Air Navigation School, RAF Hullavington

Dec 1951 – Accidental damage (Cat 4), but repairable

Oct 1952 – To 19 MU RAF St Athan

Apr 1954 – To RAF Hemswell for filming (*The Dam Busters*)

1955 – Sold to Vickers-Armstrongs, Weybridge

1956 – Presented to Royal Aeronautical Society

1972 – On permanent loan to RAF Museum

1981 – Returned to original B Mk X configuration

(Wellington history compiled by the RAF Museum with additional research by the author)

3. De Havilland Mosquito
Built in 1948 as a B Mk 35 by Airspeed (Christchurch)

VR803

Jan 1948 – Awaiting collection from Airspeed factory

Jun 1948 – Issued to 22 MU, RAF Silloth

Feb 1951 – To de Havilland for conversion to PR35 standard

Feb 1952(?) – To 38 MU, RAF Llandow

Jul 1952 – To B Flight, 58 Squadron, RAF Benson

Mar 1954(?) – To RAF Hemswell for filming (*The Dam Busters*)

(No further information available on Aircraft Movement Card as to the fate of this aircraft)

(Mosquito history compiled by the RAF Museum with additional research by the author)

4. Vickers Varsity
Built in 1953 as a T1 by Vickers-Armstrongs, Weybridge

WJ920

Feb 1953 – Bomber Command Bombing School, RAF Lindholme

Apr 1954 – RAF Hemswell for filming (*The Dam Busters*)

Mar 1956 – 20 MU, RAF Aston Down

Jun 1958 – No 1 Air Navigation School, RAF Topcliffe

Feb 1960 – Central Flying School, RAF Little Rissington

May 1960 – SRIM

Mar 1961 – Vickers-Armstrongs for modification

Jan 1962 – 4 Flying Training School (FTS), RAF Valley

Mar 1962 – 5 FTS, RAF Oakington

May 1964 – Accidental damage (Cat 4), but repairable

Jul 1965 – 5 FTS

Jan 1967 – British Aircraft Corporation, Weybridge, for reconditioning

Nov 1967 – 5 FTS

Oct 1974 – Struck off charge. To RAF Finningley for fire fighting

(Varsity history compiled by the RAF Museum with additional research by the author)

5. The Aircrew in the Film

Avro Lancaster

83 Squadron

F/Lt Ken Souter – pilot

Sgt J. Worthington – flight engineer

F/Sgt Joe Kmiecik AFM – pilot

Sgt Duncan Cameron – flight engineer

Sgt Eric Quinney – pilot

Sgt Bill Parry – flight engineer

97 Squadron

F/Off R.W. Lambert – pilot

Sgt Dennis Wheatley – flight engineer

F/Sgt T. Szuwalski – pilot

Sgt Mike Cawsey – flight engineer

Vickers Varsity

Bomber Command Bombing School

F/Lt Birch – pilot

Vickers Wellington

F/Lt Scowan – pilot

Index

Air Ministry 15, 34, 70
Aircraft:
  Airspeed Oxford 89, 90, 137
  Avro Lancaster *12*, 15, 17, 21, *21*, *22*, 23, 25, 26, 28, 30, 35, 43, 64, 65, *66*, *66*, 67, 68, *70*, 71, *71*, *72*, 77, 79, *79*, *80*, 82, 85, *85*, *86*, 87, 89, 90, *90*, 91, 93, 95, *95*, *97*, 98, *99*, 100, 101, *101*, 102, *102*, 103, *103*, 105, *105*, *107*, *108*, 111, *111*, *113*, *114*, 115, *115*, *116*, 117, 118, *118*, 119, 124, *127*, 128, 130, *130*, *132*, 133, 135, *135*, *136*, *137*, 149
  Avro Lincoln *13*, 63, 64, *64*, 65, *66*, *85*, 87, 89, 90, 99, *105*
  De Havilland Mosquito *77*, 79, 81, *90*, *137*
  De Havilland Tiger Moth *90*, 109
  English Electric Canberra *77*, *85*, 87
  Hawker Hurricane 38, 67, *67*
  Supermarine Spitfire 23, *24*, 25, 38, 67, 71
  Vickers Varsity 70, 85, *85*, *86*, 87, *88*, 89, *97*, *98*, *107*, 109, 119, *148*
  Vickers Wellington 67, 70, *76*, 79, 81, 82, 85, 86, *86*, *95*, 100, *102*, 119, *132*
Anderson, F/Sgt Cyril 28, 41
Anderson, Michael 7, 11, 15, *15*, 41-2, *44*, *50*, 51, 83, 89, 117, 119, 121, 133, *139*, 140, 141
Appointment in London (film) 33, 55, 57, 70, *72*, *73*
Associated British Picture Corporation 34, 37, 41, 42, *44*, 45, 59, 64, 70, 83, *99*, 102, 105, 117, 121, *124*, 125, 128, 135, 143, *145*, 146

Baker, George *54*, 57
Barr, Patrick *59*, *77*
Battle of Britain 51, 67
Best, Richard 33, 42, 83, 121, 133, 135, 140, 147
Blackwell, George *86*, *104*
Bouncing bomb ('Upkeep') 11, 19, *20*, 21, *21*, *22*, 23, 25, 26, 28, *49*, *69*, 72, 73, 79, 81, *86*, *122*, *126*
Brickhill, Paul 11, 34, *36*, 37, *37*, 38, *39*, 41, 42, 45, *145*

Cameron, F/Sgt Jock 65, *65*, *89*, *91*
Cawsey, Sgt Mike 65, *65*, *75*, 82, 89, 91, *91*, 92, *100*, *103*, 108, 118
Cheshire, Leonard 35, 41
Clark, Robert 41, 45, 140
Cochrane, AM The Hon. Sir Ralph 30, *31*, *37*, *39*, 44
Cold War 11, 65

D-Day 32, 35, 45
Dam Busters, The (book) 11, 34, 37, *37*, 38
Derbyshire Peak District *93*, *107*, 117
Derwent reservoir and dam, Derbyshire 25, 79, 93, *93*, *95*, *97*, 99, 101, *101*, 102, 107, 117
Desert Island Discs (radio) 149

El Alamein, Egypt *31*, 149
Elstree Studios 44, *44*, 125, 126, *126*, 133, 147
Empire cinema, London 14, 144
Enemy Coast Ahead (book) 11, 17, 33, 34, 35, *36*, 37

Far East 33, *64*, 76, 146
Fell, Sgt James 53, 57, 68, *70*, 90, 92, 101, 105, 114, 118, 119, 140
French, Sgt Bill 104, 109

Gibraltar Point, Lincs 49, 117
Gibson, W/Cdr Guy 11, 17, 18, *18*, *19*, 22, 26, 27, *27*, 30, *31*, 33, 34, 35, *36*, 40, 45, *46*, 47, 53, 55, *58*, 61, *61*, 62, *62*, 66, *73*, 79, 119, 125, 135, *135*, *136*, 140, *140*, 143
Great Escape, The (book) 38, 40

Hancock's *Half Hour* (radio) 51, 55
Harris, ACM Sir Arthur 30, *31*, 33, 44, 125
Hillier, Erwin 14, 83, 84, 88, 102, *107*, 121, 146
Holland 17, 25, 95, 108, 117
Hopgood, F/Lt John 26, 28, *52*
Humphries, F/Lt Harry 37, 40, *140*
Hutchison, F/Lt Bob *27*, 62

Inspector Wexford (tv) 54, 57

Jones, Robert *86*, 89, *104*, 121

Kerr, Bill 50, 53, 55, 57
Kirkstone Pass, Cumbria 99, *100*, 117
Kmiecik, F/Sgt Joe 65, *65*, *66*, 67, 68, 79, 87, 89, 90, *91*, 111, 114, 120

Lake District 66, *97*, 99, *100*, *107*, *115*, 117
Lake Windermere 79, 93, *97*, 99, 103, 107, *107*, 117
Lambert, F/Off Dick *12*, 65, *65*, 67, 68, *68*, *69*, 87, 100, 109, 118, 120
Langdale Chase Hotel, Cumbria *97*, *107*
Leacock, Philip 33, 70
Lincoln, Lincs *92*, 109, *113*, 118
Lincoln Cathedral *118*, 119

McCarthy, F/Lt Joe 26, 66
McGee, SAC Raymond 45, 55
Malayan Emergency 13, 65, 99
Maltby, F/Lt David 27, *54*, 57, 66
Martin, F/Lt Mick 27, 44, 47, *51*, 53, 79, 143
Mathieson, F/Lt 89, 98
Maudslay, F/Lt Henry 27, 28, *101*
Ministry of Information 34, 146
Munro, F/Lt Les 26, 66

National Physical Laboratory, Teddington *122*, 124
Nigger (dog) *59*, 61, *61*, 62
North Africa 38, 67, *67*
North Sea 17, 26, 92

Old Vic Theatre, London 48, 57
Operation 'Chastise' 23, 25, 28, 79, 107

Photo-reconnaissance 23, *24*, 25
première of *The Dam Busters* 143, *144*, 145

Quinney, Sgt Eric 67, 68, 71, 82, 87, 93, 99, 111, 115, 117, 133

RAF 15, 31, 117, 119, 120, 143
  Bomber Command 18, 23, 25, 30, 33, *37*, 57, 118, 120, 148
  Fighter Command 35, 109
  Museum 81, *86*
  Airfields:
      Anthorn, Cumbria 82
      Aston Down, Glos 68, 82
      Benson, Oxon 23
      Biggin Hill, Kent 82
      Coningsby, Lincs 87
      Hemswell, Lincs 13, 45, 55, 57, 63, 64, 66, 67, 68, 72,
      80, 82,87, 89, 98, 114, *114*, 117, 118, 120, 121,125,
      132, *136*, 146
      Kirton-in-Lindsey, Lincs 83, *99*, 109, 111, 114
      Langham, Norfolk 109
      Lindholme, Yorks 120
      Lossiemouth, Moray 92
      St Mawgan, Cornwall 68
      Scampton, Lincs 18, 25, 26, 30, *32*, 44, *51*, 53, 55, 57,
      61, *61*, 66, *69*, *77*, 82, 83, *84*, 87, 89, 90, 92, *92*, 93,
      108, 109, 114, 117, 120, 121, *122*, *124*, 125, *129*,
      146,
      Silloth, Cumbria 82, 83, 114
      Syerston, Notts 83
      Upwood, Hunts 90
      Waddington, Lincs 120
  Miscellaneous units:
      Bomber Command Bombing School 85
      CIU Medmenham *136*
      Film Production Unit 148
      1 ITS 109
      School of Maritime Reconnaissance 68
      20 MU 68
      230 OCU 90
  Squadrons:
      43 67, 67, 83, 84, 85,
      83 35, 64, 65, 66, 67, 68, 69, 70, 71, 98, 120 ,
      97 63, 64, 64, 65, 66, 67, 104, 120,
      106 18, 35, 73, 79,
      617 11, 17, 18, 18, 23, 25, 28, 30, 31, 32, 34, 36, 37,
      39, 43, 47, 57, 68, 79, 87, 102, 105, 117
Reculver, Kent 25, 117
Redgrave, Michael 15, 34, *47*, 48, *48*, 49, *49*, 51, 53, 55, 77, *125*,
138, *139*, 141, 147
Rendell, Ruth *54*, 57
Rolls-Royce Merlin engines 97, 132, *137*, 149

Ruhr dams, Germany 11, 17, 23, *24*, 25, 26, 28, 30, 31, 34, 35, 43,
102, 107, 117, *126*
      Diemel 26, 43
      Eder 25, 26, 27, 30, 35, 43
      Ennepe 26, 28, 43
      Lister 26, 43
      Möhne 17, 23, *24*, 25, 26, 27, 28, *28*, 30, 35, 43, *52*, *86*, *93*,
      126, *127*, 128, *135*, *136*
      Sorpe 25, 26, 28, 30, 43

Saracen's Head Hotel, Lincoln 118, 119
Second World War 11, 33, 57, 66, 146, 147
Shaw, Robert 57, 59, 115, *116*, *130*, 133
Sherriff, R.C. *40*, 41, 42, 45, *139*, 140
Sinclair, S/Ldr W.C. 68, *69*
Skegness, Lincs 48, 92, 117
Souter, F/Lt Ken 55, 65, *65*, 66, 67, *67*, 87, 90, 97, 98, 102, 107,
108, 111, 120, 146
Spafford, P/Off 'Spam' 57, *127*
Stewart, Val 86, *88*, 107
Stock, Nigel 57, *127*
Summers, Mutt *59*, 81, 82
Szuwalski, F/Sgt Ted 55, 63, 65, *65*, *66*, 67, 79, 87, 91, *91*, 92, 99,
108, 111, 114, 115, 119, 120, 146

Taylor, Gilbert 14, 83, 84, 86, 88, *88*, 95, 98, *98*, 102, *107*, 121,
130, 148
Todd, Richard *6*, 7, 14, 15, *15*, 34, 41, 45, *46*, 47, *47*, 48, *49*, 53,
55, 57, *58*, 59, *59*, 60, 61, 62, 93, *110-1*, 115, 116, *116*, 120, *122*,
130, *130*, 133, 134-5, *136*, *138*, *139*, *140*, 141, *143*

Vickers-Armstrong 19, 49
Victoria Cross 30, 35

Wallis, Barnes 11, 18, 19, *20*, 34, 42, 44, 48, 51, 53, *122*, 125,
140, *145*
Warwick, Norman 86, *88*
Wheatley, Sgt Dennis 65, *65*, 68, *69*
White Hart Hotel, Lincoln 61, 119
Whittaker, Bill 42-3, 61, 83, *86*, 119, 133, 140
Whitworth, G/Capt Charles *15*, 44, 108, *122*, 145

Young, S/Ldr Melvin 27, 28